COMFORT
THOSE WHO MOURN

COMFORT
THOSE WHO MOURN

**HOW TO PREACH
PERSONALIZED
FUNERAL MESSAGES**

KENN FILKINS

COLLEGE PRESS PUBLISHING CO., Joplin, Mo.

Library of Congress Card Number: 92-75784
International Standard Book Number: 0-89900-602-7

DEDICATION

Dedicated to Carol, my wife, through whom God
comforts me when I mourn.

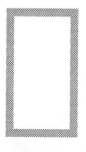

ACKNOWLEDGEMENTS

I am indebted to many people who contributed to this book.

My warmest thanks to . . . .

Dr. Paul Kissling, of Great Lakes Christian College, Lansing, Michigan, for seeing a need for this book and offering an insightful critique of the manuscript.

Leroy Filkins, for his overwhelming encouragement when I needed it most, and for his massive technical help with the electronic manuscript. Sometimes there is no friend closer than a brother.

Joyce Farrow and Cheryl Filkins, my sister-in-law, for reviewing the manuscript and for their comments on syntax and grammar.

My many friends in the ministry, such as Justin Shepherd, Ray Merritt, Rod Nielsen, Bob Palmer, Tim Sipes, Scott Taube and many others who have shared their experiences and insights on funeral messages.

My wife, Carol, and my two sons Micaiah, "Mack," and Andrew, "Drew," who not only understood when I needed time to write, but also encouraged me to do so.

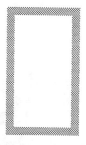

TABLE OF CONTENTS

INTRODUCTION:
About This Book

Funerals. Some ministers dread them, others fret over them, all ministers preach them. Most struggle to make them comforting. Though they're not easy, funerals come with the territory — often unexpectedly and inconveniently.

One weekend my schedule ran like this: two wedding rehearsals on Friday night, two weddings on Saturday, a young adults' party Saturday evening, preach three sermons on Sunday, teach a Bible School class, a potluck dinner, and a leadership meeting Sunday night. I knew it would be a hectic weekend. I didn't know that two families would call and I would also speak at two funerals on Saturday.

In my first ministry I quickly learned two things: ministers will preside at funerals, (the only questions are how many and how difficult) and the "canned" funeral sermons are as palatable as inviting an Italian family to dinner and serving generic spaghetti from a can. In my struggle to make every funeral as personal as possible I found several obstacles to overcome and no resources to guide me. So I learned the hard way — trial and error. Today I still wrestle to make funerals personal and comforting, but after years of experience I understand better how to write and present funerals that comfort the mourners. This book is the resource I never had.

In the following pages, we will journey through the steps in preparing personalized funerals. First we will grapple with why stories of the deceased touch people so deeply. Then we will see how to interview the survivors to gather personal stories and memories. Next we will consider organizing the biographical material into a funeral format. Following that we will discuss sharing the Gospel in a variety of funeral settings. In "Funeral for a Funny Lady" we will cover when to use humor in a funeral and when humor is harmful. We will also discuss death and "the will of God" and its relationship to people who were bitter with God for "taking my child from me." Then we will share practical suggestions for dealing with several of the most difficult funeral situations; suicides, infants, teen deaths, abusive parents, and bitter people. We will close with practical suggestions to involve Christians in the ministry of follow-up after a funeral.

All the anecdotes in this book come from real funeral situations, either from my experiences or from other ministers. No story has been fabricated to illustrate a point. As a result the stories you read about today may be the circumstance you find yourself in tomorrow.

I offer these experiences simply as a fellow pilgrim on the journey to better ministry. Along the way I will share my failures and mistakes, so that you may avoid some of the rocky roads I blundered down. I will also share some victories, so that you can see how God can use a willing heart to comfort those who mourn.

1

PERSONALIZED FUNERALS:
Stories That Comfort

"Every morning a crane lifted the construction workers in a metal cage to their work stations hundreds of feet above the street," announced the anchorman on Chicago's 6:00 news. "Today, during the lift, the cage broke and the four men fell to their deaths. At this hour many questions remain unanswered . . . ."

The live video showed the scene; police barricades blocked the gawkers, news crews interviewed eyewitnesses, construction workers sat stunned, and everyone asked these questions, "How could this happen? Weren't there any inspections or safety precautions?"

The tragedy touched me though I was 60 miles

away in the northern Indiana town where I ministered. Little did I know that I would soon be thrust into the middle of this tragedy.

One of the men who fell had lived a few blocks from the parsonage where I resided, during my first full-time ministry. The following morning the director of the funeral home called and asked if I would preside for the funeral of Charles Fredrick "Fred" Houseknecht. Though his family was associated with the congregation, I had never met Fred. His wife was a member of another church but her minister declined his funeral because Fred also belonged to the Masons.

That December day I learned how one death can affect a community. Fred, I found out, was a popular person, a member of the volunteer fire department, and active in community affairs. Everyone empathized with his young widow and two grade-school children. The whole town responded with cards, flowers, letters, food and visits. Everyone knew this funeral would gather people from every segment of our community: businessmen, school leaders, teachers, civic leaders, police officers, members of every area church, and a host of unchurched people. This death had touched the heart of our community — his youth, health, and popularity, meant that none of us were beyond death's grip.

THE PANIC

My few previous funerals for elderly people had

completely consumed my attention. This one however, had me stricken. Frankly, I panicked. "Fred was young and *should* be alive," they said. What would I say? How would I address the accident? I searched my books on funerals but found no help.

Driving to the Christian bookstore, I scoured the ministerial section. The funeral guides, with their poems, "canned messages," suggested scriptures, and written prayers seemed so impersonal. From talking with people that day, I knew that they would attend Fred's funeral because of what he meant to them. They would gather to say good-bye and to remember how Fred effected their lives. I wondered if an impersonal message, no matter how eloquent, would be heard.

Driving back empty-handed from the bookstore, I decided to interview Fred's family and friends to find out why everyone was so touched by him. Looking back, I see my clumsy attempts to glean the personal details were responded to warmly, even by his grieving widow. More haphazardly than not, I stumbled onto the stories and details that made the funeral message personal and powerful.

At the funeral the next day, family and friends packed the auditorium, lined the hallways, sat near speakers in the waiting rooms, and stood listening from the foyer. In the message I said that I learned how Fred knew no strangers and relayed anecdotes of the times he had helped others. During the stories, I saw the recognition in the audience — they remembered too. Fred's elderly neighbor's eyes brightened as she remembered how he helped her with a flat tire. Firefighters nodded as they recalled how Fred fought fires with them. Aunts and uncles smiled as they recollected Fred playing with his two children. They each had *their* story to tell about Fred. Their hearts opened, healing had begun.

After telling how Fred had helped others, I shared how Jesus' death, burial and resurrection could help us. Seeing my inexperienced attempts at a personalized funeral message now, I realize that God can sometimes use a willing, sympathetic heart, better than a classic oration.

FROM IMPERSONAL AND IMPOTENT . . . TO PERSONAL AND POWERFUL

In her booklet, *Healing Grief*, Amy Jensen advised survivors on the value of personalized funerals:

> Consider, however, that a service tends to benefit the survivors, most of whom will receive some healing from it. A funeral or memorial service can do more. It brings the support of friends and community. It gives you a goal, a stabilizing objective in those first uncharted, emotional days. And it provides for a last, loving tribute, a public declaration of love.
>
> Be involved in the planning if you can. Choosing music and speaker brings a sense of control and makes the service more meaningful. It is better to have an old friend speak with tears than an

unknown clergyman speak with eloquence.

I agree. But practically speaking, as a minister you will often be the only spokesman. Yet, you can tell *their* stories for them with great effectiveness. Personalized funeral messages comfort the family, begin the healing process and build a bridge between the speaker and audience. This bridge enables you to introduce Jesus both during the funeral and later in their homes.

Since Fred's funeral, I have labored to make every funeral as personal as possible. Many situations — such as funerals for non-Christians, abusive parents, and bitter people — make personalized funeral messages a challenge. Yet, the most effective ministry results from personalized messages, not "canned sermons."

For example, when my wife's grandpa McDowell died, we drove from Iowa to Michigan for his funeral. Because the McDowells had no church affiliation, the funeral director had suggested a person to give the funeral. The family had asked if I wanted to preach the message but thinking I was too close to the situation, I declined. After all, I needed comforting too.

At the funeral, the speaker finished in four minutes. He mentioned grandpa's name only once, in passing, and read a "canned" prayer from a booklet. The family was shocked. We felt hollow, empty, even cheated. Stunned, we stood in a small group. As we gravitated toward the casket, a pain which I did not understand wrenched my stomach. My wife's eyes portrayed an agony that I had never seen before. Her eyes asked me to do something, anything . . . .

I breathed a silent prayer, and asked the family to gather in a circle. As we stood, arms intertwined in front of the casket, I spoke of grandpa and what he meant to me. I mentioned the whitetail deer he shot — illegally — out his kitchen window while drinking his morning coffee. I commented that he lied about his age to enter the military and to serve in World War I. In China during the war, he fought "our guys," with boxing gloves in a ring. Grandpa also held dozens of patents for his inventions and he had traveled all over America collecting stones for his Rock Shop. In tears I recalled how he had given me some of his tools. "Every man should have tools," he had said. I acknowledged that I had the tools, but still could not use them. Then I spoke of our pain and loss, then of Jesus, who could heal our grief and give hope. I closed with prayer and we left for the funeral dinner.

That day I learned personally, of the comforting power of stories. No one pretended that grandpa was perfect; we knew his faults and loved him anyway. I realized that personalized funerals need not be long nor elaborate to be loving, effective and comforting.

Personalized funeral messages are not detailed biographies including every fact of the deceased's life from birth to death. They are a recollection of the stories and details that sum up his life and remind the survivors of their relationship with him.

HOW ARE PERSONALIZED FUNERALS OUTLINED?

You can present personalized funeral messages in three basic formats: a *sermon format* using personal anecdotes for illustrations, *eulogy format* where the person's life mirrors the Christian message, or the *eulogy/sermon format* which delivers the personal profile and sermon as two separate parts of the message.

The sermon format. If the deceased was a Christian, you may preach a sermon and illustrate it with anecdotes from the deceased's life. Judy Phillips was a godly, 92-year-old lady. For her funeral I used I Thessalonians 1:2,3, and spoke of her "work of faith," (her church work, including teaching Bible School), her "labor of love," (cooking for funeral dinners and at Christian summer camp), and her "steadfastness of hope," which I illustrated with stories of Judy's faithfulness in tough times.

COMFORTING TOUCH — When speaking of the deceased in the funeral sermon use his or her first name or nickname. Use the name the friends use.

The eulogy format. Sometimes a Christian's life shines so brightly that recounting it preaches the

Gospel. Even as the Hebrews writer said of Abel, "through faith, though he is dead, he still speaks." Katie Wild's example of faith, compassion and witness told so clearly the hope we share in Jesus, there was no need to preach following her profile. Her life preached it. For example, one day an insurance lady visited Katie about purchasing a policy. Katie told her, "I don't know anything about insurance but let me tell you about Jesus." The insurance lady, now a Christian, attended the funeral.

The eulogy/sermon format. This useful format works for the widest variety of funerals. It resembles a British funeral where the message is divided into two sections. First you share the biography — the eulogy — and follow it with a sermon. Think of the first section as opening the listeners' hearts and the second section as introducing a friend — Jesus — who will comfort them and give hope.

WHY PREACH
PERSONALIZED FUNERAL MESSAGES?

Diana McKendree wrote of the benefits of a funeral in her booklet called, *The Spiral of Grief*:

The funeral service helps us focus on the person who has died, the life they led and the continuing impact they have on our lives. It is an opportunity to participate in a ritual and a rite of passage, which enables us to begin letting go. Without this, our process of acceptance may be prolonged and difficult. As hard as it may be, seeing the body offers us the opportunity to say good-bye, helping to bring the relationship to a close.

McKendree mentions the three major reasons people attend funerals: to say good-bye to someone they love; to pay their "last respects" to someone who influenced them; and to remember the impact of their relationship with the deceased. Understanding these three areas will guide you in preparing messages that are relevant and healing.

Funerals are a formal time when we say good-bye to someone we love. My grandpa Atkins died after he spent a year and a half in a Florida nursing home drifting in and out of reality. For me saying good-bye meant dealing not only with the loss of the only grandparent I ever knew, but also wishing I could have talked to him one more time.

Though I am not fond of the term, "last respects," it does illustrate why some people attend funerals. When Walter Trune, an elderly Christian from my home congregation died, I attended his funeral. To my surprise so did my brother and sister-in-law. Afterward, we shared what Mr. Trune had meant to us and talked about visiting his sheep farm, playing in his barn and eating around his table.

Funerals are also a time to remember the impact the deceased made on our lives. Jeff Emerson was a young Christian man with a heart disease that mandated a heart transplant. When Jeff died before they could operate, my wife Carol and I attended his funeral. Jeff had lead her to Christ, involved her in the High School youth group and taught her the Word of God. I cried too, that day and thanked God for his witness to the lady who has become my partner in life and ministry.

THREE WAYS TO
MINISTER TO THE MOURNING

Understanding why people attend funerals enables you to select comments that comfort the family, even through your public message. No funeral sermon will ever replace the need for private counseling, visits of compassion, meeting the physical needs of the grieving and follow-up after the funeral. But funeral messages can be a catalyst for healing of the family, in at least three ways.

Funerals provide perspective on problems that the death leaves behind. As a minister you can provide God's perspective on situations like a wounded relationship with an oppressive father, or a bitter mother who *never* told her son she loved him, or the loss of a baby. We will address these and other difficult circumstances in Chapter 7, "Tough Funerals and Funerals for Tough People."

Funerals allow you to introduce Jesus. Isaiah 61:1,2 records Isaiah's prophecy that Jesus would "bind up the brokenhearted" and "comfort all who mourn." Though you will not offer an invitation hymn, you can plant the seeds for a later harvest.

24

Ken Wilkins ministered to Ethel Quiggle, when her husband was terminally ill. After the funeral Ken continued contact with Ethel and her son George, who accepted Jesus and became active members of the congregation I served. We will discuss practical tips on this in Chapter 4, "Sowing Seeds or Driving Stakes?"

Personalized funeral messages begin the healing process through stories of the deceased. Often at funeral dinners, people come up to me and say how the stories in the message reminded them of *another* story of the deceased. As I stood near the dinner line after Min Fordyce's funeral a friend of the family said to me, "I wish I would have talked to you before the funeral . . . You mentioned that Min loved animals; well, she loved turtles and horses too. I lived a half-mile from them and took over all the big turtles to Min and she made them into great turtle soup. And she had this horse . . . ."

THE DYNAMICS OF
THE PERSONAL STORIES

People are touched by the stories of other people. Books, newspapers, and magazines are full of stories about people. They are stories of trauma, tragedy, or triumph. People read about them to find answers, direction and inspiration for our own lives.

Think about the power of stories. Remember how the greatest teacher taught the mysteries of the Kingdom? With stories. Stories of farmers, shepherds, children, flowers, fish, seeds, and doves. Jesus *showed* the Kingdom's message through stories.

Luke 15 records Jesus telling stories of a shepherd and sheep, a woman and coins, and a father and his sons. Just mention "The Prodigal Son" and images of Jesus' story jump to life. You can see the dust fly from the son's Corvette Chariot as he wheels away from the father's house. You can smell the perfume of the blondes that sit at his side. Moments later that fragrance is replaced with the stench of pigs and we feel the hunger as he longs for swine food. Even stronger images rush out as we watch the father run to greet his smelly, unkempt son. The son who realized that he left the father's house and broke the father's heart. He was sorry. Then comes the images of the celebration party. We hear the music and smell the roasting beef, also we see the sour demeanor of the brother who refuses to celebrate. We learn that people can be in the father's house but not in the father's heart, a lesson his younger brother traveled far to learn.

Now contrast that story with Matthew 21:28-32. Telling the same parable, Jesus said that a father asked his two sons to work in his vineyard. One said "yes," but did not go. The other said "no" but later he changed his mind and went to work.

Which passage is the most popular? Why? Details. *Personal* details.

STORIES TOUCH US

Stories of people we have never met can touch us. When I began Judy Phillips' funeral, the funeral director went to his office to wait for the closing prayer. After he heard the audience laugh, he returned to the back of the auditorium and listened to stories about Judy. The message included stories about pancakes, and meals for grain thrashers. On the way to the cemetery, he mentioned that he enjoyed hearing about Judy.

If people are interested in the lives of others they have never met, how much more so are they interested in stories of loved ones?

"Time alone will not heal your grief," Diana McKendree wrote in The Spiral of Grief. "You must give yourself permission to fully experience it and to accept that death is a part of life. Your memories help you relive the life you shared. They can never be taken away from you and they are your gift to carry into life."

What do people talk about at funeral dinners? Stories and memories of the deceased. They are what they enjoy and what begins the healing process.

Marjorie Gordon wrote about the loss of her 25-year-old son in "The Grief Connection" (Christian Standard, August 11, 1991). In it she suggests sending stories to the grieving family to comfort them. "Write about a special moment. Like medicine for our broken hearts were the letters from Dave's friends. Many were from people we hadn't seen in several years. Some we had never met. Each searched to get our new address. Word pictures beginning, 'I remember when Dave and I . . .' recounted special moments that brought laughter and tears as we read them."

From the times I have written such letters about my friends, I know the healing that came after I wrote the family. Sharing the story comforts the heart of the teller as much as the receiver.

Why are the stories of the deceased so important to us? Maybe because they are all we have left. We may still have the fishing pole that grandpa gave us. Or the photographs of our vacations. Or grandma's rocking chair. But these items are important because of the memories they hold. The fishing rod reminds us of the summer day he gave it to us and how he loved fishing with his grandkids. The squeaking chair reminds us of grandma rocking and singing us to sleep.

STORIES HELP US DEAL
WITH THE STAGES OF GRIEF

I do not know why personal stories touch people so deeply and provide such healing, but they do. Stories of the deceased guide us through the aspects of grief, such as shock, denial, silence, anger, guilt, sadness and depression.

When my grandfather died I found that preparing for the funeral helped me stumble through the first steps of healing. Recounting stories of family reunions moved me past the paralysis of shock. Sharing with loved ones at the "viewing times" and seeing his body in the casket, directly confronted my denial. Memories of his teasing all the grand-kids guided me as I dealt with sadness and depression. All the funeral activities: the visiting, the stories, the recollections and the funeral sermon itself confirmed my loss. Before the funeral I knew intellectually he was gone. After the funeral emotionally I felt it. The memories were still vivid, there was more healing ahead, but the funeral told me it was time to move on. The funeral helped me accept his death.

My experience was not unique. Consider Lois Duncan's story from "Funerals Are for the Living," (*Woman's Day*, March 4th, 1986):

> I went over to the casket and looked down at my mother-in-law. To my surprise, I felt in control of my emotions. I had grown used to the figure in the box — and to the fact that it was only the shell that once had encased a person I loved. I felt a bond with others who had gathered to say good-bye. In three days, we had traveled together through the stages of grief — shock, denial, out-rage, bitterness — and had come, at last, to the final one: acceptance.
>
> My husband and I returned home and fell back easily into the normal pattern of our lives. Every time I went to the mailbox, it seemed strangely empty. I kept thinking of things to share with my mother-in-law, particularly news about her grand-children. I felt frustrated by my inability to send her messages. I did not, however, awake shrieking her name in the night. And although my husband dreamed about his mother often, the dreams were

not painful. They were, instead, pleasant inter-
ludes of nostalgic reminiscence in which Mom
baked his favorite pie or played the piano at a
family gathering. He was able to enjoy his memories for what they were — treasured recollections
of times that would not recur.

SOME DILEMMAS OF
PERSONALIZED FUNERALS

Though personalized funerals are powerful and
effective, they offer some inherent dangers and
dilemmas. Whenever you share personal details
you run the risk of making a mistake.

The most risky funerals are those of people you
have never met. You may wonder how to share
personal details of people you barely knew? How
do you deal with funerals of non-Christians, and
be honest yet comforting? Or, how about funerals
of bitter, spiteful people?

In the chapters that follow we will address these
and other dilemmas of personalized funerals. At
this point be assured that preparing personalized
funeral messages is not as hard, nor does it take
as long as you may think. In one eight day period,
I preached seven funerals. The first was of a "sus-
pected" murderer, who was killed when his car ran
off a cliff after a high-speed chase with the California Highway Patrol. The last of the seven funerals
was for a teenager who was hit by a truck while
delivering the daily paper. He was *my* paperboy.
During those days my blood pressure would shoot

up every time the phone rang — I wondered if it meant another crisis situation.

RESULTS OF PERSONAL FUNERAL MESSAGES

Funerals are opportunities to meet the needs of grieving families. As an ambassador of Jesus, you can bind up the brokenhearted and comfort those who mourn, then trust God to cause the growth. Note that Jesus empathized with mourners. He cried with Mary and Martha outside Lazarus' tomb. In Nain, He visited a widow who lost her only son. To Jairus He spoke words of comfort after he heard news of his daughter's death. And when He comforted Jairus' mourning family by raising his daughter from the dead, He told them to tell no one. He had more concern for their grief than His own popularity. What is more important to us at funerals, the impression we make or the compassion we share with a grieving family?

For a preacher the results of personalized funeral messages include: high visibility for the church, prospects to follow-up and eventually new members. Yet I hope no minister treats funerals as an opportunity to create a prospect list or as a public relations time — for the popularity and influence of his ministry.

But, like it or not, funerals put you in the spotlight. There are few times when you will be more public than at funerals. In them you represent not only yourself, but also the church and Jesus

Christ. The compassion, empathy, and relevancy of the funeral message — and the surrounding events — will determine greatly how people feel about the local church and its relationship with the community.

Sometimes your efforts to comfort the mourning will take years to bear fruit.

When I met with the Fred Houseknecht's widow to gather the personal details, her sister-in-law told me, "Do not preach a sermon." I smiled, nodded to her but never answered her. I thought she meant the toe-stomping sermons — the kind that make the most well intentioned Christian feel inadequate. Sermons where the preacher sounds like a witch hunter rather than a wanderer who has found his way and shares it with others. Looking back I wonder if she was not angry with God for taking Fred from them. In the message I shared the hope of Christ in an anecdotal, conversational style. Her coolness after the funeral told me she disliked the "sermon."

A few years later she and her husband entered the church after an evening service and both were in tears. Months before he had fallen while building a house and the injuries had kept him from his police work. While he had healed physically, he still struggled with self-confidence. For help they turned to Christ and His church. Later, they accepted Christ and after he had helped build the new church building, he regained the confidence to return to work with the Indiana State Police.

Other times the results of funerals are more

immediate. Before church one Sunday, I observed a new young couple. During the greeting I recognized them, but did not know why, so I said "You look familiar . . . ."

"Well, we should!" Scott Reinhold snapped. "You did my grandfather's funeral Friday."

They had heard the personalized funeral for Chester Scott, were comforted and decided to visit the church.

Jolted by his abruptness, I mumbled a thank you to them for visiting the church. As I walked away I wondered if I would ever see them again. I did, the next week. And the next. Several months later after a lot of teaching, Scott and Debbie were baptized into Christ.

They became active in the church family, spent a huge number of hours building the church building, and Scott became an elder in the church. Today our friendship endures though I now serve in another state.

Now let's see how to gather the stories and details that make funeral messages personal and powerful.

2

GETTING PERSONAL:
Interviewing the Family

The lack of specific knowledge of the deceased often keeps ministers from preaching personalized funeral messages. Gathering personal details can be awkward especially if you have never done it before, or if the family's relationship with the deceased was a painful one. This awkwardness, however, is frequently resolved by understanding the healing that an interview begins for the family. Take the case of "Kevin" and "Michelle" for example.

After the funeral director notified me about the funeral for Kevin's mother, I called Kevin and Michelle to set up an appointment. I had never met his mother.

"I'd like to stop by," I began, "and discuss what you want for the funeral service."

"We just want a short, impersonal service," Michelle said.

I sensed tension in her voice.

"Would you mind if I visited with you and Kevin about it?" I asked.

"If you wish," she replied. "How about 1:30."

That afternoon, we sat in the sunroom of their retirement home that overlooked a lake. They both were over seventy years old, but didn't look it. Kevin's mom had died in her nineties.

"Thank you for taking time to see me today," I said. "I want to learn your preferences for the service and to share how I deal with the message."

"We just want a short, impersonal service," Michelle told me, repeating what she had said over the phone.

"Could you tell me why?" I asked. "I would like to share some personal details and stories about your mother in the first half of the message."

"Kenn, I don't want to sound disrespectful to my mother," Kevin began. "But she really wasn't a very nice person."

He paused.

"I still don't understand her," Michelle said. "Kevin is 74 years old and his mother *never* told him that she loved him or gave him a hug or a kiss. She never expressed any love or appreciation for anything we did for her. I tried to treat her right — at times I'm sure — just for *my* conscience sake." She paused as a tear trickled down her wrinkled cheek.

"I cut her hair for 53 years," Michelle continued. "In all our married years we have had birthday parties and special dinners for her in our home. For all those and the Christmas, birthday and Mother's Days gifts we gave, she never said one word of thanks. Not one. Until . . . ."

She wiped the tear from her cheek.

"Until," Kevin added. "Two weeks ago."

"Yes. Two weeks ago," Michelle continued. "After I cut her hair she *thanked* me. I couldn't believe it."

"We don't want you to mention any of this," Kevin said. "And we don't want to speak ill of her but she was a bitter person. She was an avid reader and knew a great deal about her favorite subjects like crafts, nature, rocks, wildlife, and needlepoint. But the truth is she cared more about those things than she did people."

"Kevin's maternal grandmother did not hug or kiss either, but at least she was a kind person," Michelle added.

"My paternal grandparents *did* hug and kiss," Kevin said. "So I took after them. Whenever any of my grandkids come into this home the first thing they get from grandpa is a hug and a kiss on the cheek."

That afternoon, Kevin and Michelle taught me that interviewing the family can accomplish more that just gathering details for a funeral message. It can be therapeutic for the mourners. Losing a mother meant that Kevin and Michelle must cope with the loss of someone they loved *plus* the loss of any hope of healing that relationship. They had always hoped that their love would be acknowledged and returned. Now that hope was lost.

For most mourners verbalizing their memories helps them sort out their feelings. Most express feelings of sorrow, loss and love. Others deal with feelings of anger; toward their loved one who "abandoned them" or at God for "taking their loved one from them." Widows often share their fear of coping with life without their mate.

Most of the time mourners will share good memories. If hurts exist they often cover them. Sometimes they will even *shade* truth to make the deceased or their relationship with him or her, appear better than it was.

From my experience, I think that people who share painful details about the deceased seek some resolution of their feelings. Kevin and Michelle where not gossiping about his mother, nor were they spewing out their hatred; they sought to resolve their pain and loss.

A CATALYST FOR HEALING

After interviewing hundreds of families I have learned that most families *want* to talk about their loved one and that sharing those memories can become a catalyst for healing.

Mike and Jo Jones lost their son, Pat, in a construction accident caused by a tornado. When I heard about Pat, I drove to Indiana to visit them. They said that their friends would talk to them but avoid mentioning Pat's name. Though speaking of him often brought tears, they *wanted* to talk about their memories of him. Sharing these stories with others was a release valve for their bottled-up grief.

Mike and Jo shared this advice for friends who want to comfort a mourning family: don't be afraid to mention the deceased by name — it's on their minds all the time; ask about details concerning the deceased's life — your curiosity shows you care; and don't worry about always saying the "right thing" — your compassion and concern are comforting.

Most who grieve feel that way.

At times interviews begin awkwardly or slowly but once one family member shares his or her memories the rest of the family soon follows. This sharing guides them as they sort out their memories and put them into perspective. In the interview a mother may realize how her son or daughter is coping with the loss. The reverse is often true. When this happens the interview becomes a catalyst for the family's healing as they continue to share memories and feelings.

Interviews may also reveal situations that need your attention later. Kevin and Michelle's circumstance is one example. In such cases make a mental or written note to follow up on that situation. A few weeks after the funeral I visited Kevin and Michelle.

Fortunately, interviews are rarely as traumatic as theirs.

WHOM, WHEN AND WHERE TO INTERVIEW

Whom do you interview? Immediate family usually: the spouse, children, parents, brothers, sisters, and grandchildren. At times you will include cousins, aunts, uncles, friends, church members, neighbors, fellow employees, or schoolmates.

For the interview, meet with as many of the family members as possible. Meet them either at their home or at the funeral home. Ask the funeral director who the family contact person is, then talk with him or her to set up a meeting. Tell the contact person the reason for the meeting and ask when it would be most convenient. Ask him to invite the family and others, who want to help plan the service.

You may be tempted to meet with the family in a hospital room immediately after the death of a loved one. It seems like a convenient time, since they are all together. Resist the temptation. At least wait until the next day. Give them some time to deal with the shock of the loss.

I try to attend the "family-viewing" — the time when the family first sees the deceased in the casket before the public-viewing time. I often interview the family between the family-viewing and the public-viewing.

Whether or not you attend the family-viewing will depend on your relationship with the family and *their* desires. If you attend it, don't be pushy or intrusive. Family-viewings are sensitive times. They are not the place for lectures on death or pious platitudes. A warm handshake, a hug, or a tear can bring more healing than sharing the theology of suffering. "Weep with those who weep . . . " Paul said.

Ministers who preform many funerals a year can become somewhat numb to the pain of the families. That's what Justin Shepard said happened to him, until the day that his father died. Justin said, "With my father's death God jolted me and softened my heart to the pain that grieving families experience. Now, I view their pain with more empathy."

At the family-viewing, keep a low profile. At first let the family members comfort each other. When they go to the casket for the first time, stand to the side and observe. Your compassion of *presence* is the important action. The New Testament word for comfort (*parakletos*) means "to call along side" or to ask someone to stand with you. To a certain degree comfort means presence. So be ready if they need you. Often the family will ask for comfort with a look of pain. Other times they will walk over and begin talking with you. Allow them the opportunity to seek you out.

CONDUCTING THE INTERVIEW

At an appropriate time, gather the family around a table or pull some chairs into a circle.

Take along your Bible, a pen and paper to record the details. Begin the interview by offering words of condolence and comfort, read a Bible passage, and pray. Then tell them your approach to funeral messages and what details you need from them.

> COMFORTING TOUCH: Never use the words "always," "usually," and "normally" when you talk about what should be done in a funeral service. There is nothing "usual" about losing a loved one. "Others have lost mothers too, but no one has lost your mom."

"For the message," I tell them, "I'll spend the first half talking about your mother. Friends and family will attend the funeral to remember her and what she meant to them. If you tell me details about her background and life, I'll share them. But first, tell me the things *you* want to see in the service?"

Once they respond to that question, ask about music, special songs, hymns, and other people — who they want to pray, sing, or have speak about the deceased. Make notes of these points, then confer later with the funeral director.

Then ask about Scripture readings, the funeral dinner, committal service, closed or open casket, and other memorial services — such as American Legion or Masons.

THREE GUIDES FOR INTERVIEWING

Here are three points to remember when interviewing the family: don't ask questions that solicit

"Yes" or "No" answers; don't settle for generalizations, ask for details; and don't pry for curiosity's sake.

Don't ask questions that lend themselves to "Yes" and "No" answers. Don't ask "Did your mother like flowers?" Instead inquire "What were her favorite flowers?" "On what occasions did she receive them?"

In Janice Franzen's book, *The Adventure Of Interviewing,* she suggests these phrases to encourage a response.

"Tell me about it."

"How did it happen?"

"Tell me the circumstances."

"Could you give me a story or anecdote to illustrate that point?"

Don't settle for general answers. Ask for more details with follow up questions. If the family says, "He loved the outdoors," ask what specific activities he enjoyed. "Did he take his grandchildren fishing?" "What kind of fish did he catch?" "Where did he go fishing?" "How about camping?" "Where did he go boating?" "Did he have any unusual situations when he went boating?"

Janice Franzen, in *The Adventure of Interviewing,* began her chapter on "Sparkle-adding Anecdotes — And How To Get Them," with this about anecdotes:

Anecdote: from the Greek an-(not) and ekdotes (given out or published). Originally an informal or private tale, but today, according to Webster's New World Dictionary, "A short entertaining account of some happening, usually personal or biographical."

I love anecdotes . . . .

Through the use of dialogue, description and action, anecdotes paint little scenes that enable the reader to vicariously live the situation being described.

They add color. Excitement . . . .

Later in that chapter she included this anecdote about gathering anecdotes. It's from her interview with Franklin Graham as she prepared a magazine article.

"Your mother, it is said, has a terrific sense of humor. Did that help lessen the stress between you and your parents?" I asked. That, it turned out, was the key question, although I didn't know it beforehand. It opened a floodgate of memories.

"My mother would do some crazy things that would irritate me," he said, "For example, when I was living at home and attending a junior college, I often would want to get up late because I'd been at a party the night before. I had an old tin cup that I used as an ashtray. I never smoked in front of my parents, only in my room. So the cup would fill up with cigarette butts and ashes.

One morning my mother tried to wake me up, but couldn't. I had my door locked. So she went to my brother's room, crawled out on the roof, came through my window, picked up the tin cup, and dumped all the cigarette butts on my head . . . So mother was a character . . . .

Don't pry for personal details for curiosity's sake. Don't pry into areas that the family obviously doesn't want to talk about. The interview is no time to seek juicy tidbits for your personal curiosity. It's a time to comfort the family by listening to them. Also, it may be tempting to interject your own personal comments. "Well, that story reminds me of when . . ." Resist the temptation. Let them talk.

ASK QUESTIONS FROM FIVE CATEGORIES

When interviewing a family you will find that these categories will guide you to a comprehensive interview. The five categories are: Personal, Professional, Family, Favorites, and Faith. Let's take each area and demonstrate what kind of details to seek.

PERSONAL TRAITS:

Begin with questions about personal details about his or her childhood and personality. I have found that it's easier for the family to begin with this information rather than a more sensitive area like family relationships.

Ask questions like, "What stories did he enjoy telling about his childhood?" If you get a story that begins with, "When I was a kid, I walked four miles to school through snowdrifts up to my eyeballs . . ." Use it; many will recall him telling it.

Ask about where they lived, the house they grew up in, and their school/college activities. Ask about the deceased's relationships with her neighbors. In Mona Williams' biography I mentioned the following details which described her relationship with her neighbors when she wintered in Florida.

Jim Burr was Mona's neighbor in the Pine Island neighborhood. He said:

> Mona was the Mayor of Pine Island. And if people were sick or in need, I told them, "Call Mona; she always holds up under the pressure." To one lady who was sick I said, "Wait here, I'll get Mona; she's half doctor." Once a neighbor in Florida was cut while working on his home and Mona held off bleeding until help came.

When one of Mona's sons had rheumatic fever and was home for six months the Doctor said, "I usually put boys like you in the hospital but this time Mona will take care of you."

Also ask, "How would you describe what kind of person he was?" "Was he outgoing or reserved?" "Can you think of a story that shows that?" When you ask these questions, you will occasionally find a unique story of the deceased which demonstrates his character trait. With this story I took Paul Harvey's approach.

> It was Christmas Eve and a man was walking down a busy street. The wind was so cold it would bite through your best winter coat. Even so, the snow glittered in the street lights. Everyone on the street was so excited, so busy. Hurriedly they tried to accomplished their last minute shopping for the celebration. In all their hurry no one noticed a little girl standing in the cold, gazing through a store window at a display of pretty dolls.
>
> She was shaking from the cold and poorly dressed with a dirty face. Her parents didn't have the money for warm clothes much less to buy gifts like the bright dolls she admired through the window.

46

In all the hurry and scurry no one noticed her. No one that is, except one man. He asked her first name and what she was looking at, then bent down to gaze into the window with her. He didn't just wish her "Merry Christmas" and walk on. He took her in and bought her the doll and a winter coat then asked for her address and took her home.

As the man steps away from the little girl's door, we notice the familiarity of his gentle voice and as he turns to shield his face from the wind, we see by the street lights a glimpse of his face. We know this man . . . It's Tom McGovern.

PROFESSIONAL BACKGROUND:

The second category of questions is professional details. Ask questions about his life's work, how he chose it, and his relationship with co-workers. "What was the first job he ever had?" "Who did he work for next?" "What stories did he tell about working there?" "Why did he start in that line of work?" "What details did he mention about his fellow employees?"

After asking the children of George Miller those questions, I wrote this capsulation of this 95-year-old's early life and professional activity.

"George's life spanned from the time of the horse and buggy to the horseless carriage, human flight, man on the moon and the home computer age.

"His grandparents came to LaPorte, Indiana in 1836 (148 years ago — 60 years after the signing of the Constitution of the United States of America in 1776). Their occupation was that of coopers —

barrel makers.

"George was born in 1889 and he married Gladys McQuiston in 1916. They were married some 50 years before she passed away.

"During the advent of the automobile, George worked in the garage where LaPorte's first car was kept. He chauffeured its owners everywhere they went. When the local veterinarian had an emergency, George would take him to the farm in the car. When cars became more popular, George would go and stay with each farmer for a week to teach him to run the car."

Also under the Professional category, ask about any volunteer work the deceased did: volunteer fire department, hospital visitation, service club or children's home.

Question the family about the deceased's military service. Carol's grandfather McDowell — who fought in WWI in China and spent most of this time boxing in the ring with other servicemen — is one example of a military anecdote.

In one interview, I learned of one man who served in the Navy during WWII and slept on ship beside parts of the A-Bomb which shook Japan and left an irrevocable mark on 20th Century history. In his profile I mentioned it.

FAMILY RELATIONSHIPS:

Next ask about the deceased's relationships with the family. When they give you a general statement like, "She loved her grandkids very much," ask how she *showed* her love for them. "What activities did she do with her grandchildren?" "Did she take them to the park?" "Did she have a special dessert she made for them?" "Did she make handmade Christmas gifts for them?"

When I spoke at my grandfather Atkins' funeral, I mentioned how he always teased us grandkids. When one cousin brought home a blonde boyfriend for the first time, grandpa would say, "I thought your boyfriend had *red* hair."

"Remember how grandpa teased us?" I asked during the funeral. "That was his way of saying we were important to him and that he loved us."

Also ask about the deceased's relationships with his/her spouse, children, grandchildren, parents, siblings, and other relatives — aunts, uncles, cousins, etc. Focus here on stories that show relationships.

In Tom McGovern's funeral I shared this anecdote which described the relationship between Tom and his stepdaughter:

> The love that Tom received is typified with this clipping from the Herald Argus newspaper from earlier this month.
>
>> "They say to have a real father is one of the best joys in life for a girl. But I want to say, having a STEPFATHER like you, Pop THOMAS McGOVERN is better than anything in this world. HAPPY 28TH ANNIVERSARY to you, Mom and Dad. I love you both dearly.
>>   Your Daughter, Brenda Pierce"

At Nellie Williamson's funeral I shared these details which demonstrated Nellie's relationship with her family.

> Nellie had dreamed about being a teacher. This love for teaching she transferred to her daughter Patti, who is now a high school teacher.
>
> Patti mentioned that the first thing she remembers is her mom telling her Bible stories. Nellie also made up stories to tell. These stories had the same animal characters day to day and they became serial stories of sorts.
>
> Nellie took her grandmothering calmly. Patti tells of one day at the park, when Mark wore his sandals and climbed to the top of the Jungle Gym. Patti was on pins and needles and alerted Nellie to the danger. Nellie simply looked up from her book and said, "Oh, he'll be okay." And calmly went back to her reading.

When preacher Justin Shepard interviewed the Grubaugh family he asked them, "What was the most important thing about your father?"

Almost with one voice they replied, "Sugarbush." Sugarbush, Justin quickly found out, was an acreage in northern Michigan, where the family often gathered. They relayed many special events that took place at this wooded family property — including making syrup from the sap of its maple trees. Most of the important events for this family happened there.

For the funeral Justin wrote a poem entitled "Sugarbush." It detailed many of the family's memories of the special place and reminded them of the relationship with the man whose vision and compassion made that acreage their respite. Because I'm not a poet, I simply *talk* about the specialness of such places and recall the family's memories.

FAVORITES:

Next ask questions about the deceased's favorite activities and items. Ask about the deceased's favorite songs, artists, poems, poets, books, and authors. If for instance, someone's favorite music group was *Kansas* you might include a quote from their hit song "Dust In The Wind," about the brevity of life. The Apostle Paul did something similar by quoting a Greek poet in his message at the Areopagus in Athens —Acts 17:28.

If you know a favorite book or author you may be able to include a quote in your message.

In the interview with Joseph Bealor's family I learned this story concerning his favorite author.

"Joseph enjoyed reading Westerns — most of all Louis L'Amour books — of which he has a considerable collection," I said at his funeral. "Joe's daughter-in-law recently bought him a Western novel (not written by L'Amour) and a couple days later he told her that it didn't have a lot of action in it. To Joe, she replied, 'When I opened that book there's a lot of dust, thumping of hooves and gunfire coming out of it.'"

Ask questions about favorite activities such as hiking, skiing, sewing, knitting, fishing, hunting, boating, baking and gardening.

Ask questions like, "Did she enjoy gardening?" If you find that she loved to garden and often gave away her tomatoes to family and friends, then mention it. Most of the audience will remember eating her tomatoes.

Mona Williams' family shared this anecdote about her love for fishing with her husband and some friends.

"Mona, Paul, Joe and Ruth would go trolling for walleyes in Canada. They used a lure called a Flat Fish. One day Mona's lure had half of the hooks missing and most of the paint off. When they asked if she wanted another one, she said that her lure was fine. She kept catching fish and even caught more than the men."

When I learned for George Miller's family that his favorite hobby was photography I wove that fact into his biography like this:

George also worked for Kramer & Son Grocery for 38 years. Then later he worked for Moore's Camera Shop — photography was George's chief hobby. He enjoyed its calmness, relaxation and creativity. For several years he gave his time as a public servant; he ran the 16mm projector for the Public Library. George traveled to the County Home, Westville Correctional Facility, and various nursing homes to show films. This type of servanthood was what Jesus talked about.

FAITH:

The fifth category of questions is about the

deceased's faith in God. Of course, your questions here will depend greatly on whether or not the deceased was a Christian.

Ask about her favorite Bible verse, book of the Bible and hymn. If you learn a Christian's favorite Bible verse, share it in the message and seek to illustrate how it affected her life and how it should encourage us.

Joan Persinger was a godly lady in the congregation I served in Rolling Prairie, Indiana. The first time she was in the hospital with cancer, her in-laws visited her. They wondered how they could comfort her, instead they found that Joan comforted *them*.

"Everything will be fine," Joan told them. "After all we're just foreigners in a strange land. We're just passing through." In her memorial service I told this story and read Hebrews 11:13-16 which she had alluded to.

Ask about church membership and their involvement in the church's body-life. "Did they lead worship, sing special music, teach VBS, or work on building churches?" Ask about the times they mentioned God, Jesus, the church, or Heaven. In all these categories seek out details that will encourage the mourners.

When interviewing Mona Williams' family one son gave me a poem called, "I Needed The Quiet," which Mona had picked up at church over 25 years before. It demonstrated her faith in God and the fact that she was going "home." The last stanza of this anonymous poem reads:

I needed the quiet, no prison, my bed,
But a beautiful valley of blessing instead,
A place to grow richer, in Jesus to hide —
I needed the quiet, so He took me aside.

Before Cora Kadolph died she told her preacher, Justin Shepard, to preach at her funeral about "God's great white handkerchief, that will wipe away every tear from our eyes." When Justin did, it became an opportunity to share Cora's faith in Heaven and in God's grace, compassion and comfort.

When Dean Trune spoke at his father's funeral he shared this story which illustrates Walter Trune's faith and obedience to God.

"Obedience. I remember receiving a call at work from Gary Hawes (the Director of the Michigan Christian Campus Ministries) on March 19th, 1984 and being challenged to make a change from engineering to campus ministry. In the process of seeking God's will, I went over to my father's house and asked him what he thought I should do. If he said that he thought that I should stay with General Motors, then I was ready to do just that.

"I didn't get an answer from him at first but simply a lot of questions. Finally, I was convinced that I was not going to get an answer so I decided to leave. As I was standing on his porch ready to descend the steps to my car, he made a statement that I will remember the rest of my life. He said, 'If that is what God wants you to do, then you had better do it.' God powerfully worked through my father in giving me direction on a difficult decision. It was simply, 'Obey God!'"

Near the end of the message Dean said, "After a trial year in the campus ministry, I again approached my father to seek direction. When asked what he thought I should do, this time there was no hesitation. He resolutely said, 'I've had you around here for 35 years, it is time to let you go.' For my father, we had him around for 80 years, it is time to let him go. Oh, Death where is your victory? Oh, Death where is your sting? For my Dad, Death lost . . . Jesus won."

RELATE, REHEARSE AND RECALL . . .

Think of the interview in three stages: Relate, Rehearse, and Recall. First you *relate* with the family by comforting them, being a friend, and being there. Next they *rehearse* memories, stories, and details of the deceased with you during the interview. Then, you *recall* those memories with the friends and family at the funeral.

In the funeral message your goal is to share personal details and stories to show the essence of the deceased's life — not give a play-by-play account of every year. How do you decide what details to include and which to leave out?

Next, we'll discover how to organize and present the personal profile in Chapter Three.

3

PRESENTING
PERSONAL PROFILES

Every person's life is significant. God created him in His image and God loved him — even if he never responded to God's love. And Jesus died for him; a substantial price for a valuable person.

His family loved him, then they lost him. Now you will stand before them and in a brief message capsulize his whole life — his joys, defeats, trials, sorrows, victories, relationships and faith. For a few minutes his *life* (not his eternal destiny) will be in your hands.

In this chapter we'll discover which details to select from the interview and how to organize them into a personal profile (also called a biography or a eulogy).

First, let's see how the biography fits into the whole funeral service. The biography is to the funeral what a family room is to a home. A family-room contains family portraits, snapshots, comfortable furniture and family memorabilia, and a personal profile contains memories, word pictures and comforting stories of the deceased.

AN OVERVIEW OF A FUNERAL SERVICE

Each funeral service has three basic sections — the introduction, the personal profile and the sermon. The introduction examines the occasion of the funeral, the profile focuses on the deceased, and the sermon declares the hope we have in Christ.

Visualize the introduction as the porch of a home, the biography as the family room and the sermon as the dining room. A funeral message without the Gospel is like inviting a family to your home and getting acquainted with them in the family room then sending them away *empty*. A funeral sermon without a biography is like skipping the family room, going straight to dinner table, then staring at each other — like strangers seated together at a fast-food restaurant.

The following chart displays *one* of the many ways to outline a funeral service. You can build on this foundation and adjust it to fit the needs of each funeral.

OVERVIEW OF A FUNERAL SERVICE

INTRODUCTION SECTION:
    Special Music — sung or instrumental
    Scripture Reading
    Introductory Paragraph
    List of Survivors
    Prayer
    Special Music — sung or instrumental
PERSONAL PROFILE:
    Biography of the Deceased
    Transition Statement
SERMON:
    Assurance of Life in Jesus Christ
    Closing Prayer
    (Invitation to Funeral Dinner)

INTRODUCTION SECTION

The introductory section examines the occasion of the funeral — "why we're here." Like the porch of a home, the introduction allows everyone access to the front door and the house. It is also their first impression of the home.

Selecting Special Music. Some families want no special music, others desire congregational singing, and many request either instrumental music or that a song be sung. When selecting special music choose songs that are meaningful to the deceased or significant to the family. Before Luella Albee died of cancer, she had asked her teenaged granddaughter, Dawn Witt, to sing two songs for the funeral. Dawn had sung "Love Lifted Me" and "This World Is Not My Home" to her while Luella was bedridden. Because singing at the funeral was too emotional for Dawn, she recorded the songs on a tape and we played them as an introduction to the service.

Selecting Scripture Readings. For the opening Scripture readings you can read the text for your message or some other passage about God's comfort, Jesus, the resurrection or heaven — passages like Isaiah 40:1-8, John 14:1-6, Isaiah 61:1-3 and I Thessalonians 4:13-18.

The Introduction Paragraph. This paragraph explains "why we're here" — to remember the deceased and our relationship with him or her. For Earl Williams' funeral, I used a straightforward introduction.

"On this Tuesday in February, we pause from our work, our busy schedules, from many important duties, from the general hurry and scurry of life to remember . . . .

"To remember one who was to us . . . a husband, a father, a grandfather, a neighbor, a friend and a Christian brother . . . .

"Earl Isaiah Williams."

List of Survivors. Next I continued with a list of the deceased's survivors and started the sentence with:

"Earl leaves behind his wife . . . ."

Then I named the survivors beginning with the closest relative — his spouse, children, parents, grandchildren, and siblings. When you find unusual names that are difficult to pronounce, ask the funeral director or a friend of the family. It is important to pronounce the names correctly.

Though some ministers think that mentioning the survivors is "old-fashioned," I found that it lends a personal quality to the service.

Prayer or Special Music. The list of survivors is sometimes followed by a prayer or special music. Your preferences and the family's desires will guide you in this.

The Profile of the Deceased. Next comes the biography of the deceased. The profile can be presented in three different formats: it can be the whole funeral message (when a Christian's life proclaims the Gospel), the sermon only format (where the text is illustrated with anecdotes from a deceased Christian), and eulogy/sermon format which presents the profile and Gospel separately (this is the most useful format especially for non-Christians).

Transition Statement. This is the anecdote or paragraph which leads the listeners from the family room into the dining room — from the profile to the sermon.

Promise of Life in Jesus Christ. In Chapter Four we'll discuss how to present the Gospel in a conversational style to the non-Christian funeral audiences.

Closing Prayer. Close the funeral service with a prayer for God's strength and comfort for the family. At times the family will request that you invite the audience to the funeral dinner. If so, simply invite them to share with the family to offer their encouragement.

HOW TO SELECT DETAILS
FOR THE PERSONAL PROFILE

When you create a personal profile you will glean details from four areas: your interview with the family, your knowledge of the deceased, writings of the family, and "outside resources" — such as poems and quotes. Let's see how to select material from each area.

DETAILS FROM THE INTERVIEW

Your interview with the family and friends is your richest resource for the profile of the deceased. Select stories and details which highlight a specific aspect of his or her life. In Theresa Pointon's profile I shared these details which highlighted her determination and her desire to learn. They were from the the *Personal Category* of the interview.

"One day Theresa drove their model 'T' car up an icy knoll, only to have it slip and slide back down the hill, where the car wound up backwards in the road. After she got it stopped, she simply slipped it into reverse and *backed* it up the hill. She was ahead of the game with front-wheel drive cars . . . .

"Theresa enjoyed music and good books. She also loved to learn. She strained to learn several new languages, including German, Polish, Spanish and Lithuanian — her dad's native tongue. She did all this through her own study . . . ."

For my father-in-law Vic Bierschbach's funeral I shared these details which demonstrated his diverse *Professional Background.*

Vic was a salesman and an entrepreneur all his life. In Rose City where he grew up, he ran a gas station then moved to Lansing to work at Oldsmobile and run another gas station. Over the years he sold cars, real estate, motor homes, travel trailers, and nuts and bolts. In summer he set up fruit stands and ice cream stands. He started Northland Specialties, his own nuts and bolts supply company. He operated a huge flea market on M-37. He was an auctioneer. He served in the Air Force as a radio technician. Dan said, "He also planted trees in the National Forest."

Vic started the Sparta Eagles Club and with Bill Russell, he started the Bitely-Brohman Sportsman's Club.

I wondered if this guy ever slept!

Estoria, my mother-in-law, told me of the year that her birthday and Mother's Day were close together. Between those days Vic bought her a brightly colored Mercury Comet. Her son Dan drove it to the prom and Estoria drove it once. But before her birthday arrived three days later — he sold it!

The *Family Category* of the interview revealed these details about Oscar Taylor Sr.

"Oscar was a loving husband to Martha — his wife of 54 years. During the years of her illness, he was her faithful companion as well as her eyes and hands. He had made a commitment to love his wife. Love is a commitment to *do* what is best for the other person. Oscar demonstrated that. Paul's definition of love in I Corinthians Chapter 13 rings true with Oscar and Martha.

"Oscar learned how to cook — and to cook well — during Martha's illness. She would tell him how to cook the meal and he would. He wasn't afraid of new recipes either. Two of Martha's favorites were his pies and his pork-steaks in mushroom gravy.

"Oscar fulfilled his vow . . . 'to love, honor, cherish and comfort her until death do you part . . . ' Oscar said, 'I do.' And he did."

During the months that Joan Persinger struggled with cancer, her *favorite* hymn was "It Is Well With My Soul," by Horatio Spafford. Surprisingly, that hymn was written after Spafford had lost all of his daughters to a storm at sea. Later, as he sailed across to Europe, he wrote these words when the ship neared the spot where the storm had taken his daughters.

> When peace like a river attendeth my way, When sorrows like sea-billows roll, Whatever my lot, Thou hast taught me to say, "It is well, it is well with my soul."

From the *Faith Category* of the interview with Nellie Williamson's family I selected this story:

> Any account of Nellie's life would be incomplete without mentioning her faith in God and Jesus Christ as her Savior. Her faith was demonstrated by her daily prayers for her family. When Nellie lived with Patti's family, her room had an intercom

connected with the rest of the house. Nellie prayed her evening prayers aloud and one night she mistakenly left on the intercom. When Nellie prayed for each family member in detail, her love poured out with every word. One family member mentioned that it humbled her to hear Nellie's positive prayer for her.

Much later, Patti told Nellie about that night. Nellie was a little shocked at first then said, "Well, now you all know, how I feel about you."

So far we have only discussed positive stories but what if you find some negative details? Let's say you knew that the deceased had been in prison. Do you share that part of his profile? It depends.

Did the deceased demonstrate that God can be victorious even over his failure? Will God receive the glory for the story? Or, will the family feel threatened by the details? You have to weigh these items one situation at a time. If, for instance, the deceased had told me about his prison time and relayed how God gave him the strength and grace to conquer his struggle, I would talk with the family. If they agreed then I would share that story.

DETAILS FROM YOUR
KNOWLEDGE OF THE DECEASED

The second richest resource for the profile is your relationship with the deceased. In previous chapters, I mentioned my personal comments at the funerals of my grandpa Atkins and Carol's grandpa McDowell. But personal comments from the minister are also appropriate when you're not related to the deceased. Consider this example from Marguerite Prestin's funeral profile:

> On a personal note, I agree with many others who said that, Al and Margy easily befriended people. They befriended me. Less then two months ago, I visited the Prestin home to deliver a cookie and candy basket from the church's Senior Saints' group. While we visited, Al told me about his past hunting experiences and how they both loved wild game. After I heard that, I promised to bring them a wild rabbit, when my trained hawk caught one. Fortunately my hawk bagged four rabbits the next day. When I arrived at their house, they had just returned from one of their daily drives . . . .

In Joan Persinger's profile I mentioned this story which demonstrated the love between Joan and my oldest son, Micaiah:

> At church, my three-year-old son Micaiah would often sit with Joan. When she became too ill to come to church he always asked about her. One day recently, when we passed their house Micaiah said, "Joan doesn't feel good. I'm going to make her something." He was thinking of chocolate chip cookies though he couldn't even turn on the oven . . . .

When Floyd Costello, an elderly bachelor from the church died, I mentioned his friendly hand-shake, his worn and tattered Bible, and his involvement with the Senior Saints. After his funeral I received the best compliment I've ever received for a funeral. His sister told me, "Thank you for your comments. I could tell you loved him too." She was right.

WRITINGS OF THE DECEASED AND FAMILY

The writings of the deceased and of the family can offer encouragement and comfort to the mourners. For Clarence McCullough's profile I read a recent letter sent to him from his son in California. It illustrated their relationship and the son's love for his dad. At Mona Williams' funeral I read some poetry that her son, Don Williams, had written to her. Justin Shepard has written poetry for many of the funerals that he has performed. Justin takes the details (and his personal knowledge of the deceased) and weaves them into a poem to read during the profile.

In Katie Wild's profile, I read her poem "Smiles" which showed her attitude about life and encouragement. I also quoted some stanzas of Katie's poem called, "Time," which warned us to make the most of our time for Jesus.

For Vic Bierschbach's service my sister-in-law Tanja Kelly asked me to read this untitled, anonymous poem. It too focused on the preciousness of memories:

To the living, I am gone.
To the sorrowful, I never returned.
To the angry, I was cheated.
But to the happy, I'm at peace.
And to the faithful, I never left.

I cannot speak, but I can listen.
I cannot be seen, but I can be heard.
So as you stand upon the shore gazing at the
    beautiful sea, remember me.
As you look in awe at the mighty forest and its
    grand majesty, remember me.
Remember me in your heart, your thoughts,
    your memories; the times we cried, the
    times we fought, the times we laughed.
For if you always think of me, I will never
    be gone.

Sometimes the family may write a reading that is misleading. On one such occasion the reading mentioned that the deceased was in heaven. But everyone knew that the deceased had openly scorned both Christ and His church. I simply rewrote two sentences so that they expressed a Christian's hope in Heaven, not the deceased's.

OUTSIDE SOURCES FOR
THE PERSONAL PROFILE

Sometimes you can weave "outside" essays, stories and poems into the profile. Select only the materials which highlight some aspect of the deceased's personality or minister to the needs of the mourning family.

Quite frankly, most "funeral poetry" leaves me cold. So I use outside poetry sparingly. However, I have found the poem "Should You Go First" comforting and well received. Its theme? Memories, again.

Widows often request copies of it.

SHOULD YOU GO FIRST

Should you go first and I remain
    To walk the road alone,
I'll live in memory's garden dear,
    With happy days we've known.
In Spring I'll wait for roses red,
    When fades the lilac blue,
In early Fall when brown leaves fall
    I'll catch a glimpse of you.
Should you go first and I remain
    For battles to be fought,
Each thing you've touched along the way
    Will be a hallowed spot.
I'll hear your voice, I'll see your smile
    Though blindly I may grope,
The memory of your helping hand
    Will buoy me up with hope.
Should you go first and I remain
    To finish with the scroll,
No lengthening shadows shall creep in
    To make this life seem droll.
We've know so much of happiness
    We've had our cup of joy,
And memory is one gift of God
    That death cannot destroy.

                              –Anonymous

Another very useful *outside* resource is an essay
written in 1904 by Bessie Anderson Stanley of Lin-
coln, Kansas.

SUCCESS

He has achieved success who has lived well,
laughed often and loved much; who has enjoyed
the trust of pure women, the respect of intellectual
men and the love of little children; who has filled
his niche and accomplished his task; who has left

the world better than he found it, whether by an improved poppy, a perfect poem or a rescued soul; who has never lacked an appreciation of the earth's beauty nor failed to express it; who has always looked for the best in others and given the best that he had; whose life was an inspiration and whose memory a benediction.

Of course, the Bible is a resource for comforting profile support material. Do not confuse this with the Gospel sermon to follow. Here's the difference. The profile support material sheds light on this particular death or its effect on the mourners. The sermon shares the hope that Christians have in Jesus. Certainly some Bible stories do both. Consider this example from Joan Persinger's funeral:

Today we mourn the loss of our Christian sister. Some Christians feel that they should not mourn because our sister has gone to Heaven — a much better place where there's no more pain or sorrow. Surely we do not mourn as those "who have not hope" (I Thess. 4:13-18), but Christians do mourn.

Consider the words of the Apostle Paul in Philippians 2:27, where he wrote of his Christian brother Epaphroditus. "Indeed he was ill, and almost died. But God had mercy on him, and not on him only but also on me, to spare me sorrow upon sorrow." Why would Paul have had "sorrow upon sorrow" if Epaphroditus died? Because he feared for Epaphroditus' eternal destiny? Of course not.

Paul's mourning would have been for himself because he was *left behind* and separated from his Christian brother. Christians have the assurance of a grand family reunion in Heaven — but we still miss our Christian sister until that reunion day. We miss Joan because we love her . . . .

Joyce Landorf in her classic book, *Balcony People*, also wrote about this:

> Ray DeVries, the former vice-president of special service at Lexicon Music/Light Records, died of a heart attack at the age of fifty. At his funeral Ralph Carmichael, who gave the eulogy, told of the life Ray had lived . . . he called Ray his "pastor" and the "corporate conscience" of Lexicon and Light Records. But what impressed me the most, was at the very end Ralph, with tears streaming down his face, said simply, "Ray was my friend, and I'm going to miss him."
> It wasn't that Ralph didn't know he'd see Ray in heaven one day . . . it wasn't that Ralph denied Christ's victory over death, it was simply that Ray's life was so incredibly lived that the human side of Ralph (and all who loved Ray) would miss the man.

Others Bible stories relate how Jesus cared for the mourning; like His visit with the widow of Nain during the funeral of her only son (Luke 7:11-17), and Jesus weeping with the two sisters at the tomb of Lazarus (John 11:32-37).

Justin Shepard presents the story of Jesus sleeping during the storm from Mark 4:35-41 in this way:

> Jesus was with His twelve disciples in a boat on the Sea of Galilee when a brutal storm agitated the lake. While the waves swamped the boat, Jesus slept quietly on a pillow in the back. Because of the topography, even the fishermen in the group had no warning of the approaching storm. Jesus could have stopped the storm ten miles away if He would have chosen to. He did not.

Jesus allowed the storm to come so they would recognize their dependency on Him.

The disciples tried everything they could and all their human efforts had failed. Finally they turned to Jesus, woke Him and asked if He cared about their situation. Please note here that, a terrible storm could not wake Jesus but the voice of a person in need did awaken Him. Jesus then stood and spoke to the winds and the waves, "Quiet. Be still." Instantly the waves and wind obeyed Him and the disciples became afraid.

You say, "Well, thank you, Justin, for a nice Bible story. But what does that have to do with us? We just lost a loved one . . . " Well, think of this, no one will live long without a storm. If you never have a storm you may not realize how much you need Him.

This is your storm . . . Will you seek Jesus to calm it?

God sometimes calms the storms — like raising Lazarus and the widow's son — and sometimes in the midst of a storm, He calms His child.

THREE WAYS TO
PRESENT A PERSONAL PROFILE

Now that you have gleaned details from the family interview, collected your personal comments, the family's writing, and selected *outside* sources for the personal profile, how do you organize it into a presentable format?

There are three formats: the profile only format, the sermon only format, and eulogy/sermon format which delivers the profile and Gospel separately.

COMFORTING TOUCH — Write and deliver the personal profile with a "conversational tone." Speak as if you're talking with a friend over coffee in his family room. Use eye contact and create a tone that bridges the gap between you and the mourners.

As we discuss each format remember these two suggestions that apply to every format. First, consider writing a complete manuscript for the profile. Though I preach weekly from an outline, manuscripting a eulogy allows me to handle the details precisely and carefully — especially for someone I didn't know.

Secondly, don't *idealize* the deceased. Every person has faults and though you won't often mention faults specifically, don't pretend they aren't there.

If I don't know the deceased and the family appears to idealize the deceased, I start the personal profile with a statement like, "From the family I have learned . . . ."

In Walter Trune's funeral, his son Dean Trune dealt with the issue of idealizing at the beginning of the profile:

> It is not my intent to idolize my father or make him out to be something he was not . . . This is our best effort to please our father and our Heavenly Father at the same time.
>
> I would like to read the Scripture passage from Hebrews 11:11-14 . . . .
>
> The writer of Hebrews tells us that perfection is not something that we accomplish by living a perfect life, but perfection is something that is given

us by putting our faith in Jesus. My father was not perfect any more than you or I are, but he was in the process of being made perfect which comes through God's grace . . . .

Walter Trune was a common man who did common things, uncommonly well. Remember, he was not a perfect man, but he was in the process of being made perfect . . . .

Now let's examine each of the three ways to organize a personal profile.

THE EULOGY AS THE WHOLE MESSAGE

Sometimes a Christian's life shines so brightly that by sharing his or her personal biography the love and hope of Jesus radiates vividly. In such cases following the biography with a sermon seems redundant, even anticlimactic. Here are some excerpts from one example — Katie Wild's funeral.

After the introductory paragraph and the list of survivors, I read Isaiah 61:1-3. Following the scripture reading Katie's daughter-in-law sang one of Katie's favorite songs, "Shepherd Of My Heart":

Katie Wild was a godly, loving, Christian woman — a giant of a person . . . I began. When I first wrote these glowing remarks, I thought to myself that it sounds like praise we reserve for Jesus. But it shouldn't surprise us that we can use such remarks for Katie, because that's Who she wanted to be like!

Katie was a lady of many talents and deep char-

acter. She expressed her concern for others by crocheting afghans, lap-blankets and slippers for
people in the nursing home. She also made hats
and mittens for her kids and grandkids. Last year
she created handmade doilies — each had the
family's name embroidered into it. Katie also cro-
cheted a wall-hanging of the 23rd Psalm, which is
displayed here in the church.

Katie was an excellent cook especially of wild
game that Rayford brought home — but she never
ate wild game. She also enjoyed the Old Testament
and told me that she experienced it on the day
that "Ray brought home his first wild turkey and I
made it into a burned sacrifice!"

She had a generous spirit and the ability to see
needs (which others didn't see) and to meet those
needs. She provided gloves and Christmas gifts for
needy kids. When one family — whom she didn't
know — was burned out of their home, Katie "went
all out" to help them. No one knew who had helped
that family . . . .

Katie's attitude about life is shown in this poem
she wrote called, "Smiles" . . . .

Many of you here have received poetry that Katie
wrote for your birthday, family gatherings, retirement, or for the Gilmore Church. Katie's wisdom
shines through her two volumes of poetry. On
September 23rd, last year she wrote these lines
from a poem called, "Time" . . . .

Katie cherished her children and grandchildren.
She read to her grandkids book after book. She
even recorded readings for them and rang a bell
when they were to turn the page. Her home is
filled with photos of her grandkids. Katie and her
granddaughter (also called Katie), sang special
music together including the song, "Lord You Are
More Precious Than Silver." How was Katie Wild
like this? She loved Jesus (and His Church) and
spent her life striving to be like Him. She simply
let her light shine for Jesus. While most people

carry a candle, Katie carried a torch . . . .

She carried at least four torches — Love, Generosity, Encouragement and the Gospel. I already mentioned her love and her generosity. She encouraged others in many ways, including writing notes to the discouraged or depressed. Many people have mentioned Katie's encouragement as the reason they first came to this church.

Katie also carried the Good News of Jesus wherever she went. One of her favorite verses tells of Jesus standing on a hill overlooking Jerusalem and crying for its people. Did you know that Katie cried for us?

Katie's faith in Jesus gave her hope which she shared with others. On the night she learned about her cancer she said to her daughter Brenda, "If the Lord takes me tonight, I'm ready." The last time Katie was in the hospital she said to her son Grant, "Now maybe, I'll see Jesus."

Years ago, an insurance lady stopped to sell Katie some insurance. Katie listened to her for a few minutes then said, "I don't know anything about insurance but I know about Jesus. Let me tell you about Him." That insurance lady turned out to be Pat Mogg, whom Katie won to Christ.

Katie believed in the hope and assurance of Jesus. When Grant was in high school he asked, "Mom, what is heaven like?" Katie replied, "Do you know what it's like when you're running the ball in a football game and the crowd is yelling and cheering?" "Yes," Grant replied. "Then you cross the goal line and everyone mobs you?' "Yes," he said. Then Katie said, "That's what heaven is going to be like."

SERMON ONLY FORMAT

The second way to present the biographical

material is by using the outline of a Bible passage and illustrating it with personal details from the deceased.

Passages that work for this format include; I Thessalonians 1:3, I Thessalonians 5:16-23, and I Peter 4:7-11. I Thessalonians 1:3, for example, outlines into three points; work of faith, labor of love and steadfastness of hope. I Thessalonians 5:16-23 divides into one point for each verse. The Bible is full of such passages.

For instance, Katie's profile could have been organized around Proverbs 31:10-15, 20-31 and each of the points could have been illustrated like these two examples.

"Proverbs 31:13 — 'With wool and flax . . . she works with her hands in delight.' Katie expressed her concern for other by crocheting afghans, lap-blankets and slippers for people in the nursing home . . . ."

"Proverbs 31:28 — 'Her children will rise up and bless her . . . ' Katie cherished her children and grandchildren. She read to her grandkids book after book . . . ."

When I use this format, I work harder at keeping it "personal" to the deceased and family. My tendency is to slip back into a preaching mode.

Ray Vincent often used this topical approach which divides the message into three points:

Death Separates Us, But Not From Love
Death Separates Us, But Not From Memories
Death Separates Us, But Not From Faith.

Vincent speaks about the deceased's relationship with the family and friends under *Love*. For the *Memories* he shares details and stories about the deceased. *Faith* relays the assurance we share in the resurrection of Jesus.

These first two formats work best for organizing profiles of Christians and I rarely use them for non-Christians. For most funerals, I use the next format which divides the personal profile and the sermon into separate sections.

THE EULOGY/SERMON FORMAT

Though I use this format often for funerals of believers, I have found it especially functional for a non-Christian's funeral. Here, I organize the personal profile's topics and themes in a loosely chronological order.

Organizing the biography by themes gives you freedom to shape the direction of the message. For example, the order of the themes in Luella Albee's profile was; childhood, quilting, camping, cooking, marriage, farming, children, grandchildren and caring — each theme was illustrated like those in Katie's profile. Under "caring" I mentioned how Luella had cared for ill relatives in her home; these included her dad, her uncle, sister-in-law, her husband's dad and mom. Luella's caring became an easy bridge to cross to Jesus' caring.

For Earl Williams' profile the themes were his personality, military service, his "wild" animals, his family, marriage, illness (which illustrated his dependence on God), and his faith and humble service in the Kingdom.

In closing the profile I said, "In our simplest actions we reveal our character. Few people knew that Earl and Betty would come to the church (when no one else was around) to pick up sticks from the yard or repair something. They never told anyone. They just served the Lord wherever they saw a need. They expected no honor or reward — they simply served. Which reminds us of Jesus' comment, 'The greatest of you will be the servant of all . . . .'"

TRANSITION TO THE GOSPEL MESSAGE

Following each biography is the transition statement which transports the audience from the profile to the sermon.

At times, as illustrated above, the transition is connected with the last point of the personal profile — sometimes that is not easy.

If the deceased was not a Christian, don't "preach them into heaven" nor "roast them in hell." Rather, seek to save those who are left. Many times the transition statement is as simple and direct as: "The occasion that drew us all here today reminds us of life's most difficult question. If a man dies shall he live again?"

Now that you've opened the hearts of the mourners it's time to introduce a friend — Jesus

— who can comfort them and give them hope.

How do you introduce Jesus? We'll discover that in Chapter Four.

4

PLANTING SEEDS
OR DRIVING STAKES?
Sharing the Gospel at a Funeral

Ministers often view the Gospel portion as the easiest section of a funeral because its content depends upon who Jesus is, not who the deceased was. Obviously we know more about Jesus than about the deceased. But this section of the funeral can become tense if the family requests two ministers for the funeral and the preachers believe in different philosophies of funeral ministry. At Frances Hickman's funeral I saw two philosophies of funeral ministry side-by-side.

One minister viewed funerals as a time to convict the mourners of their sin, instill repentance, and badger them to submit to the Gospel. He viewed the listeners as his enemies and he used the Gospel like a sledgehammer. His words were heavy and blunt.

Time after time he attacked the audience. To him grace was a gauntlet, the Bible a belt, and holiness a hammer. His message and tenor drove a wedge between himself and the survivors. While listening my heart cried out, "Didn't Paul say, 'the *goodness* of God calls us to repentance'?"

As he spoke, I realized that he did not seek to comfort the mourners, but to convict the crowd. Several family members said afterward, "This is no time for that!" Many were repulsed. Some were angry.

They also mentioned their thankfulness for the other minister. His demeanor was friendly, confident, and warm. It showed through the tone of the message as well as its content.

He mentioned Frances' physical disability and his commitment to Jesus. I watched as he "connected" with the audience. As he spoke of Jesus, I envisioned a farmer calmly walking through a field scattering seeds on all the soil, from good to poor. He spoke clearly of a Christian's hope in Jesus' resurrection but offered no invitation. He just planted the seeds and (it appeared to me) trusted God for the harvest.

That funeral more than any other forced me to evaluate how I shared the Gospel with a funeral audience. Would I lovingly plant seeds, or drive stakes to mark the battle lines? Since then, I have committed myself to understanding funeral audiences and sharing the Gospel so that they will clearly understand it.

COMFORTING TOUCH — Focus your message on consoling the mourning family and friends. Keep your tone positive, hopeful, and compassionate by speaking of Jesus' compassion and His resurrection.

THE UNIQUENESS OF FUNERAL AUDIENCES

Funeral audiences differ from the usual Sunday congregation in at least three ways: they represent a cross-section of the community; they are hurting and exploring; and they are basically "spiritually illiterate."

A cross-section of the community. On Sunday morning we speak to believers and seekers — people who attend church either have or desire a relationship with God. But people attend funerals because of their relationship with the deceased. Therefore funeral audiences contain people from every spiritual segment of the populace — believers, seekers, atheists, backsliders, vile people, the spiritually indifferent, moral non-Christians and cult members. This diverse audience challenges us to speak in terms they understand and provides us an opportunity to share the Gospel with people who rarely hear it. As diverse as these people are, they have one factor in common — they're hurting.

Hurting and exploring. The grief a mourner feels at the death of a relative or friend forces them to face death close up — hurting often sparks exploring. In his or her own way, each strives to cope with the brevity of life and its *real* meaning. This presents a unique opportunity to plant seeds and touch lives. But not every mourner will respond to you the same way.

Some people see the minister as a representative of God — sort of an *Ambassador of Heaven*. As a visible representative of God, mourners may respond to you as they feel toward God. If for example, they are angry with God for "taking our dad" they may shun you. Others may try to appease your view of the deceased as if that will satisfy God too. In these situations, use the funeral times to show acts of compassion and build relationship with the family. That relationship may offer opportunities for teaching later.

Spiritually illiterate. Most people in a funeral audience will be spiritually illiterate. Though they have heard of Jesus, many don't understand the Gospel nor the assurance of the resurrection.

Many have misconceptions about God and Jesus. I've often heard people say, "God is loving and He wouldn't send anyone to Hell." They fail to realize that we are all lost and on a ship sinking on the sea of sin. A loving God has sent His lifeboat to rescue us. If we drown, it will be our choice — not God's.

Other people have GPS — Good Person Syndrome. "I know Johnny will be in Heaven," one mother told me.

"Why?" I asked.

"Because he was such a good person," she answered. "He always left the cherries in the tops of the trees for the birds. "

In his funeral I mentioned that we're saved by grace, not by our good deeds.

As a result of this spiritual illiteracy, it's acceptable to view a funeral sermon as *pre-evangelistic*. Use the funeral to create a positive encounter with Christianity and prepare the listener for Jesus. Studies have shown that most people have ten to fifteen positive encounters with Christianity before they respond to the Gospel. A funeral can add one more positive contact with Christians.

HOW TO REACH A FUNERAL AUDIENCE

After you have gained the attention of the mourners through the Personal Profile, introduce Jesus in the same warm, conversational and anecdotal style. Communicate compassionately like Christ did when he spoke to the leper who had asked if Jesus was willing to heal him, (Mark 1:40-41). Speak conversationally as Jesus did to the Samaritan woman at the well, (John 4:4-26). Illustrate the points with stories — stories like those Jesus told — that are simple without being simplistic.

To appeal to funeral audiences consider these four suggestions:

- Be non-threatening in your tone
- Appeal to their way of thinking
- Share personal experiences
- Keep your points simple

Be non-threatening. Treat the audience as friends to be won, not enemies to be conquered. Tactics you use to gain the attention and interest on Sunday morning may not be appropriate for a funeral. I once read of a preacher who started a funeral sermon with, "You're all a bunch of losers . . . " I trust he went on to share the hope of Jesus, but why dig a hole to crawl out of? This type of "shock statement" has value in a Sunday sermon where the audience knows you. But a funeral audience will take the statement at face value and that will make the speaker their opponent, not their friend.

Sit with them by their fire. When Hudson Taylor was a missionary in China he shaved his head and left a long braid in the back; he then encouraged other missionaries to do the same. That's what Jesus did when He "took on the nature of a man . . . " (Phil. 2:5-11).

As you prepare each funeral message ask yourself several "What if . . . " questions to help you relate to the pain of the family. Ask yourself, "What if that were my father, how would I feel?" "What if that were my sister who just died of cancer, what questions would I ask?" Asking "What if . . . " questions can draw you to some common ground with the mourners.

Note how Paul found the common ground with his Areopagus audience in Athens. He used a non-threatening, positive tone as he sought to win this secular audience. Paul "reasoned" with them in terms which they understood. Paul began "I see that you are very religious in all respects . . . " (Acts 17:22 NASB). He continued his non-threatening demeanor by appealing to their way of thinking.

Appeal to their way of thinking. Learn to see the issues from their viewpoint and answer questions that *they* are asking. One minister said that he reads the Bible and the *New York Times* every morning, "to find out what each side is doing."

After hearing Hudson Taylor speak, one Chinese man said, "You make it sound like God is a porter, who takes a suitcase too heavy for me to carry." Taylor had communicated in their terms.

When Paul spoke to the Athenians, he demonstrated that he had looked at the issue from their perspective, "while passing through and examining the objects of your worship . . . " Paul said. Next he dealt with *their* perceived need, "I even found an altar with this inscription: TO AN UNKNOWN GOD. Now what you worship as something unknown I am going to proclaim to you." (Acts 17:23 NIV).

Here again some "What if . . . " questions will guide you in understanding the perceived needs of the mourners. "If I was this non-Christian and my grade-school daughter died suddenly, how would I feel toward God? Angry? Hateful?"

Because of the Athenians' view of the Hebrew Scriptures — they rejected them as a source of authority — Paul proved his points without quoting them. Instead he quoted their sources, " . . . he (God) is not far from any of us. 'For in him we live

and move and have our being.' As some of your
own poets have said, 'We are his offspring.'" (Acts
17:28 NIV).

At a funeral you can support your point with a
brief quote or story from a newspaper or magazine, then read an appropriate Bible passage and
say, "That's what the Bible has taught all along."
Paul met the audience on their ground and quoted
sources that they trusted — like personal experiences.

Share personal experiences. Illuminate the
Gospel with personal experiences from your life
and those of other believers. Read any popular
secular magazine and you will see that non-Christians (and many Christians) consider personal
experiences as a valid basis for conclusions. Sub-
jectivity is no basis for our relationship with
Christ, but sharing personal experiences can convince unbelievers of the modern relevancy of the
Bible. Then they may examine the Scriptures as a
source of authority. Paul shared his encounter
with the resurrected Jesus as testimony to King
Agrippa, (Acts 26:12-19). At a funeral a personal
story of how a Christian deals with the loss of a
loved one can encourage mourners to consider the
relevancy of Christianity.

To illuminate how a Christian views death I
share Patricia Riesenweber's story of "The Door:"

> One day when she was 13, Patty Riesenweber
> was taking her three-year-old brother David to the
> church where their father was the minister. Patty's
> mother had sent them to bring Dad home for

lunch. To reach his office they had to pass through the church basement, a very dark and spooky place, and just before they came to Dad's door, Patty thought up a little prank.

"I'll plant David in front of the office door, knock boldly, the quickly run around the corner out of sight," she thought. "Dad will be expecting an adult and how surprised he'll be to see little David standing there."

Patty knocked on the door, and darted away. As she peeked around the corner, she could hear Dad's footsteps coming, yet through the gloom she also saw David's lower lip trembling. Only then did Patty realize what she had done to him, how frightened he was standing there alone in the big, scary basement, abandoned by his sister, listening to the heavy footsteps coming closer. Just then the door opened and he looked up into his Dad's face. David radiant with relief and joy, smiled and held up his arms. His Dad lifted him up and hugged him.

I often recall that story when I think about my own death. If ever I'm frightened about facing that door alone, I simply imagine the joy I'll feel when the door opens and I look up into my Heavenly Father's face.

–(Adapted from *Guidepost* Magazine, February, 1982, page 36.)

Also see Dr. W.W. Winter's personal story about heaven in the appendix.

Keep your points simple. Because of the spiritual illiteracy of the audience keep your funeral message simple but not simplistic. Jesus' messages were often simple yet profound.

Keeping it simple means, in part, sticking to the basics. When you discuss death, don't discuss the nuances of the time/eternity issue. Don't say,

"When we die, we leave time and enter eternity — where all time happens at the same time. Therefore whenever you die that becomes Christ's Second Coming for you. In eternity there is no time and all time happens at the same time. So when you enter eternity you can see all the events of history happening at the same time, therefore you'll be at Christ's Second Coming instantly."

Save that discussion for a Bible School class. In a funeral stick to the basics, like "death means separation."

Simple also means cutting the church jargon — speak in terms the audience understands. A normal funeral audience is perplexed by statements like, "Let Jesus come into your heart."

At the Areopagus Paul refrained from church jargon, he called Jesus the "righteous one" — a Greek poet's term — instead of the Messiah which is a Jewish term.

Edward T. Thompson, Editor-in-Chief of *Reader's Digest,* offered this advice on avoiding jargon. "Don't use words, expressions, phrases known only to people with specific knowledge or interests. Example: A scientist, using scientific jargon, wrote, 'The biota exhibited a one hundred percent mortality response.' He could have written: 'All the fish died.'"

How often do we use words like justification, sanctification, redemption, oaks of righteousness, and grace, without any definition or example of their meaning? Such actions leave a funeral audience in the dark.

FUNERAL SERMONS —
SIMPLE YET PROFOUND

Funeral sermons can be conversational without being corny, warm without being lukewarm, and challenging without being crass. Like the Apostle Paul, focus your message on Jesus and His resurrection.

Here are some excerpts from a funeral sermon called "Sleeping," that I used for an audience of unbelievers.

After the Personal Profile of the deceased I began:

> The reality of what faces us today brings to mind one of life's most formidable questions. If a man dies shall he live again?
>
> G. B. Hardy wrote, "I only have two questions: Has anyone ever cheated death? Has he made a way for me to cheat death?"
>
> The answer is, "No." No one has cheated death — that's the problem.
>
> The popular philosophy of this century claims that life is the greatest good and death is the greatest evil. They claim that this life is all we have and that death is the end.
>
> Even Shakespeare noted this despair in Macbeth:
>
> > "Out, out brief candle!
> > Life's but a walking shadow, a poor player
> > That struts and frets his hour upon the stage
> > And then is heard no more; it is a tale
> > Told by an idiot, full of sound and fury
> > Signifying nothing."
> > (Macbeth, Act 5, Scene 5)

Gladly today I tell you, there is hope. Because of

Jesus Christ and His bodily resurrection, Christians have the hope . . . the assurance of eternal life. Jesus did not "cheat death," He confronted death and the grave and became victorious over both. And He has promised that same victory to those who follow Him.

The word death simply means "separation." There are three kinds of death: physical death when the spirit is separated from the body (one day my spirit will leave my body and I will die); spiritual death, when a person is separated from God (like Adam and Eve were cast from God's presence in the Garden); and eternal death, when someone is separated from God forever.

But let's talk about life. If death means separation, then life means "union." And there are three kinds of life: physical life, when the spirit is united with the body; spiritual life, when a person is united with God (through faith in Jesus Christ); and eternal life, when a person is united with God forever — that's Heaven.

The Bible does an interesting thing when it mentions death. It often replaces the word death with the word "sleeping." The Bible does not use "sleeping" to avoid the word death or to minimize the trauma we feel to lose a loved one. Rather the Scripture uses "sleeping" for death to remind us of an important principle concerning death.

When people are asleep they are unconscious and separated from us but we don't fret or mourn, because we know that they will awaken and we'll be reunited with them. The Bible uses the word sleep to speak of Christians who die, because the separation caused by death is not a permanent one but a temporary one. Because of Jesus and His bodily resurrection from the dead, Christians have the assurance that death is not a permanent separation and we too, will share in the resurrection from the dead.

Death is not the end. It is just a door from this life to the next.

Even with the assurance of a grand reunion in Heaven, the death of a loved one is still painful. Jesus knew that. It was the evening before His own death on the cross, that Jesus spoke these words to comfort His closest followers, "Let not your hearts be troubled, believe in God and believe also in Me . . . " (John 14:1-6).

The Apostle Paul also mentioned that we will mourn for the "sleeping." But he said that we'll mourn "not as those who have no hope." In I Thessalonians 4:13-18, Paul says, "Brothers, I do not want you to be ignorant about those who have fallen asleep . . . ."

On one Easter Sunday — the day when we celebrate Christ's victory over death and the grave — Sam Stone wrote this editorial for the *Christian Standard* about the assurance that believers share in Jesus.

One young man was killed in an auto accident. His family found comfort in a letter he had written to his aunt some years before when her husband died. He encouraged her to think of his uncle's death as "a new birth into God's kingdom."

COMFORT THOSE WHO MOURN

Remember, he suggested, that his suffering is over.
He has gone on to greater things. Then he quoted
selected verses from I Corinthians 15 closing with
these words . . . (Read: I Cor. 15:54-57.)

Another tragic death was that of a young minister's wife who died in an accident at her home.
Her father, a well-known Christian minister,
wrote:

"At last, Lisa is Home. The body she lived in for
twenty-seven short years lies at rest beside a
weeping cherry tree in a Lexington cemetery. But,
Lisa is alive in Glory . . . Her mother and I are not
wealthy by the world's standard. We believe that
our greatest treasure is in the lives of the children
God has given us as a stewardship. And now, we
are grateful that this portion of our riches is safe
in His eternal storehouse." (Copyright, Christian
Standard, April 24, 1984, used with permission.)

Hope, assurance and victory are three reasons
why Christians are comforted on days like today.
Hope in Heaven because of the assurance of Jesus'
resurrection which offers victory over death and
the promise of life eternal . . . .

If the deceased was a Christian I try to close the
message with an anecdote of their faith, as George
Brown did at Wanda Timm's funeral:

"Wanda would sometimes meet me at the door
after the morning service, hold my hand and tell
me that she had enjoyed some of the sermon, but
had fallen asleep. She claimed it wasn't my sermons, but that she had had some trouble sleeping
during the night. Right now she is sleeping —
sweetly. And the Scripture promises that the Lord
gives to His beloved, even in her sleep.

"Wanda has been freed of this earthly tent, no
longer does she have to wait. She is clothed in an

94

imperishable garment. No longer does she have to struggle to sleep. She's resting comfortably, without pain, without sorrow, sleeping soundly until that clarion trumpet of God signals her to rise. And rise she will. And all who are in Christ Jesus will join her as she ascends."

TEXTS AND TOPICS

Funeral manuals suggest a vast number of suitable funeral texts including: II Corinthians 5:1-8, I Thessalonians 4:13-18 and several sections of I Corinthians 15. But topical sermons can also be effective.

After the Personal Profile, Justin Shepard shared these three points: The Characteristics of Death, The Concepts of Death, and The Conqueror of Death.

Characteristics of Death. How do people die? Some die with money, others without money; some die popular, others alone; some die old, others young . . . .

Concepts of Death. The four basic theories about death: anomalistic, "when your dead you're gone"; reincarnation, *recycling* the spirits; spiritualism, human spirits are released into a spirit world which we can contact through seances; Scriptural testimony about the afterlife, "Just as man is destined to die once, and after that to face judgment," (Heb. 9:27 NIV).

Conqueror of Death. Christ demonstrated His lordship over death when He visited three towns:

Capernaum, Jairus' daughter; Nain, the widow's son; Bethany, Lazarus.

USING BIBLICAL
STORIES IN FUNERAL SERMONS

There are many comforting Bible stories that enhance funeral sermons. As an example, consider the story of the criminal crucified next to Jesus. Jesus said to him, "I tell you the truth, today you will be with Me in paradise" (Luke 23:43 NIV). The criminal was not the top candidate for paradise but he made it, not because of what he knew but whom he knew — Jesus.

Sharing the personal experiences of people comforted by Jesus in the Bible illustrates Christ's compassion. I often tell the story of the widow of Nain to illustrate how Jesus cared for a mourning mother, especially at a child's funeral (Luke 7:11-17).

The story about Jairus' daughter depicts Christ's compassion for a mourning parent and Jesus' power over death (Mark 5:21-43). I relay the story up to the point where Jesus entered the room where the little girl laid. In the story I include: the resources the father tried before he asked Jesus, the messenger's disappointing news, Jesus' comforting words to Jairus and Jesus' confrontation with the "commotion-makers."

Then I say:

When Mark recorded this miracle he mentions the specific Aramaic words that Jesus spoke.

Jesus said, "Talitha koum." Why would Mark write the specific words then follow them with a translation, which means "Little girl, I say to you, get up" (Mark 5:41). Mark told us the actual words of Jesus to impress upon us the amazing power of Jesus over death. When Jesus raised this girl from the dead, He did not have to call on any outside powers or spirits. He just spoke to her in a language she understood and she stood up.

Jesus needed no potions, no incense, no incantation . . . Jesus didn't have to enchant the gods with a spell like, "Raz-ma-taz, Wow-pa-now, Look at me and stand up now." Jesus — as God in human flesh — didn't even have to ask the Heavenly Father for help. All Jesus did was speak and this dead girl heard the Lord of life and stood up.

USING "OUTSIDE" STORIES
TO SUBSTANTIATE THE GOSPEL

"Outside stories" come from sources unrelated to the deceased and the family. As mentioned earlier the best anecdotes come directly from the life of the deceased or the family but this is not always possible. Therefore, I use "outside" stories to confirm and clarify the Gospel, like Patty Riesenweber's story, the letter from the nephew and the quote from the father in Sam Stone's Easter editorial. On occasion I'll share one of these anecdotes from Dwight L. Moody. The first demonstrates assurance and the second exhibits victory.

Dwight L. Moody once said from the pulpit, "One day you will read in the obituaries that, 'DWIGHT L. MOODY is dead. When you do, don't you dare believe it. Because I will never be more alive then on that day!"

Voltaire was an infidel of the most profound type. He said, "I wish I had never been born!"

Lord Byron lived a life of pleasure. He wrote, "The worm, the canker, and grief are mine alone."

Jay Gould, the American millionaire, when he was dying said, "I suppose I am the most miserable man on earth."

Lord Beaconfield said, "Youth is a mistake, manhood a struggle, and old age a regret."

Alexander the Great conquered the whole world then wept and said, "There are mo more worlds to conquer."

When the Evangelist Dwight L. Moody was on his death-bed in the hospital, his family had gathered at the doctor's request. The doctor took the family from his room and told them that Dwight was slipping quickly.

They went back into his room and prayed by his bed for healing. When Dwight realized what was happening he said, "Don't pray that for me today. This is my Coronation Day!"

Editor Sam Stone shared this insightful anecdote about the "sting of death:"

A Christian physician specializing in allergy treatments told of a young child who nearly died from an insect sting. He was warned that another such sting could be fatal. One day when the child was riding with his father in the car, a bee flew inside. The child became hysterical.

The quick-thinking father pulled the car off the road and caught the bee in his hand. Then the child relaxed. But after a moment, his dad let the

bee go. The little boy became upset again, scream-
ing and jumping into the back seat.

"Don't worry, Son. You don't have to be afraid
anymore," his father comforted him. He pointed to
his hand, "See — the stinger is in my palm. This is
what could have hurt you. I have taken the sting
of death away."

So did Jesus.

Paul concluded the great resurrection chapter by
saying, "Where, O death, is your victory? Where, O
death, is your sting? The sting of death is sin, and
the power of sin is the law. But thanks be to God!
He gives us the victory through our Lord Jesus
Christ."

–(I Cor. 15:55-57, NIV).

We need not dread the tomb. The funeral service
is not the final farewell for believers. Reunions
await. We anticipate a better home than we ever
had here, free from every problem.

Christ's resurrection has made the difference —
the eternal difference. Our hope rests in Christ.

Death means no longer a hopeless end, but
rather an endless hope.

–(Copyright, *Christian Standard*, April 19, 1992,
used with permission.)

Minister James Postel told of a Sunday School-
class of eight year olds:

Among them was a mentally handicapped child
who had always been a part of the class but not
fully accepted by the group. Tony was "different"
and a class of eight year olds was not equipped to
understand that difference. Somehow the things
that Tony did always seemed funny, even when
they weren't.

One spring the class had been studying the
Easter story and the events leading to the Resur-

rection. On Easter morning, the teacher gave each child a large plastic egg, the kind that packages a well-known brand of hose. Each was asked to go into the church yard and find something to put into the egg which he considered a symbol of the resurrection.

When the eggs were opened, some contained flowers, some new green leaves, and others bits of grass or small plants. However, when the teacher opened Tony's egg, it was totally empty. At first the class laughed, but then they realized that Tony had caught the real symbolism of the resurrection with the empty plastic egg, as empty as the tomb.

After the incident of the egg, the class began to look upon Tony with more understanding, and he was accepted as a real member of the group. However, within a few years, Tony caught an infection which his frail body was too impaired to fight. His death was a severe blow to his parents although they had known since his birth that he would not live to maturity.

At Tony's funeral, the eight year olds marched as a class to the front of the church and stood before the casket. Solemnly they placed on it their tribute to Tony — not flowers but a single, empty plastic egg.

–(*Vidette Messenger*, April 6, 1979)

CONDUCTING GRAVESIDE SERVICES

Treat the graveside "committal" service as an extension of the funeral message — carry over the same tone and demeanor.

At the graveside be brief, to the point, and compassionate. If you have something to say, share it at the funeral service when everyone is seated and listening. At one graveside service a minister spoke for 35 -minutes while the people stood outdoors on soggy grass — they became impatient and perturbed. He had spoken for only nine minutes while the audience was seated comfortably and ready to listen.

Committal services have three sections: your comments, a reading and a prayer.

Your comments will explain "why we're here at the graveside."

"This is a place of last good-byes. It's also a place we return to which reminds us that we remember and still care . . . ."

Sometimes I explain the tradition of burying the deceased face up with his/her feet to the East, "This way when Christ returns 'from the east,' they will be facing Him when they rise from the grave."

Other times I comment on the creation of Adam "from the dust of the ground. And the body is here but his spirit is in the hands of God."

If possible I include some anecdote or detail about the deceased for the graveside service — at times this can be a reading.

The reading for the committal is a Scripture passage and (at times) some additional reading. Psalm 23 is the most popular reading, therefore I try to avoid it unless the family requests it. I prefer sections of Psalm 139, Isaiah 61 or I Corinthians 15.

For Judy Phillips' committal service I personalized it by mentioning that she had often sung special music for church and read two verses of one of her favorite hymns, "Beyond The Sunset."

Note Judy's comforting words to the family as expressed through this hymn:

"Beyond the sunset, O blissful morning,
    When with our Savior heaven is begun.
Earth's toiling ended, O glorious dawning;
    Beyond the sunset, when day is done.
Beyond the sunset, O glad reunion,
    When our dear loved ones who've gone
    before;
In that fair homeland we'll know no parting,
    Beyond the sunset, for ever more!"

A prayer closes the graveside service. Again ask for comfort for the family as they look to God and Jesus for strength. After the prayer go to the family and quietly offer your encouragement. Then step aside and allow the family and friends to share in this moment.

5

FUNERAL FOR A FUNNY LADY:
How to use humor
in a funeral message

I first met Judy Phillips when she returned to Michigan after "wintering" in Florida. In March, Ron Apple and I visited her at the farm house where she lived alone. We thought she had celebrated a birthday recently so Ron asked, "Wasn't your birthday a few days ago?"

"Yes," responded this tiny lady with a bright smile.

"Well, how old are you now?" he asked.

Her smile fell to a dead-pan glare. "Oh, you should know that you *never* ask a lady her age," Judy said as she waved a finger at him.

Ron rocked back into his chair like a third-grader reprimanded by his teacher. We had thought that a lady over 90 years old wouldn't be sensitive about her age. *We were wrong.*

After she saw the shock register on our faces and listened to the momentary silence, she laughed.

"I'm 91 years old," Judy said smiling wider than before. She hooked us and she knew it!

Over the next year I became familiar with Judy's witty, joyful personality. When she died and the family asked me to share at the funeral, I began collecting my thoughts and memories of Judy. Because of Judy's personality many of the tales about her were humorous. I wondered how I could share these details when people might laugh out-loud during the funeral message.

Would people be offended and think that I was taking their loss lightly? Or, that for me funerals were trite? Or, even that I was disrespectful to the deceased and grieving family?

Because humor was such a part of Judy's life, this funeral forced me to evaluate what humor is proper for a funeral. I knew that omitting the amusing stories and her witty statements would leave a huge void in our memories of Judy. Funerals are a time to remember what the deceased meant to us. In large measure Judy meant humor and joyfulness to us. I could not avoid humor in Judy's funeral message.

At the beginning of the message the Funeral Director checked the microphone volume and disappeared into his office. I began Judy's funeral profile with Judy's birthday story. The Director returned when he heard the laughter. He may have wondered if a verbal mistake had prompted the laughter, then he heard the next story.

Judy and Bill had a dairy farm and later raised beef cattle. When the threshers came for the harvest, Judy and the neighbor ladies would cook mounds of meat, potatoes, vegetables and (Judy's specialty) homemade pie. Judy told of one day when a neighbor lady came to help in the kitchen and took her shoes off for a while. When the lady put her shoes back on, she felt something wiggling in one toe. Judy didn't say anything. Later the lady mentioned the wiggling in her shoe again.

"Well, let me help you with that shoe," Judy said.

"When Judy took the shoe off the lady's foot, a bewildered field mouse ran out."

The lady screamed. Judy shrugged her shoulders, "It must have come in with the threshers," she said and went back to mashing the potatoes.

Judy was "a lady's lady." She always kept herself, her clothes and her hair neat and "proper." Even when she was in the hospital last month Judy asked her daughter Betty to ask the "permanent lady" to come. Judy said, "How can I get well without a permanent?"

In Florida a retired man who lived across the street from Judy called her, "Grandma," to which Judy replied, "He's too old to be my grandchild!"

At Judy's funeral people laughed and cried. The Director stood and listened to the whole message and later told me how much he enjoyed listening to Judy's stories. Her joy had touched him too.

HUMOR CAN HEAL . . .

Judy's funeral and others have taught me that

humor is not a funeral taboo, as I had once thought. Actually I learned that laughter can become a part of healing. After all, Proverbs 17:22 reveals that "a joyful heart is good medicine." (NASB).

Nick Gallo wrote in his *Better Homes and Gardens* health column:

> Like exercise, laughter reduces stress. Once laughter stops, blood pressure drops below normal for a brief period. Breathing slows down. Muscular tension subsides. The result: Most people feel a relaxing afterglow.
>
> Laughter also has a physiological effect on the body. Biochemically, laughter seems to cause the release of natural painkillers (endorphins) that combat arthritis and other inflammatory conditions. It may also slow the release of stress hormones . . . Laughter also appears to be one of the best antidepressants available. Like a ray of sunshine, it softens emotional pain, brightens outlook, and broadens perspective.
>
> COMFORTING TOUCH: Humor becomes a catalyst for healing if it flows naturally from the life of the deceased and his or her relationship with the family. The key is "from the family" — never use jokes or "canned humor" in funerals.

Like any sermon a funeral message flows through the mind and personality of the preacher. There's no separating the message from the messenger. Some preachers are at home with humor and others find it awkward. Whatever your personality you can learn to include humorous details *in some way* when the deceased's life abounded with it. Instead of telling the humorous stories you could mention the deceased's humor and list a couple items to illustrate it.

Humor crosses all geographic and social contexts. I've shared humor at funerals where the deceased and family were from urban, rural and suburban areas, and it was well received in each. The key is not the social context, but that the humor flows "naturally" from the life of the deceased. It is the difference between "natural humor" and artificial "canned humor." As with the other details you select for the deceased's personal profile, humorous stories should express an aspect of the deceased's character or display his or her outlook on life.

FUNERAL HUMOR — BALM OR BOMB?

Humor in a funeral can be a balm or a bomb — a healing salve or a painful stab. Healing humor emerges intrinsically from the personal stories, but humor hurts if it is a joke "to relieve the tension of the audience or speaker." Jokes to "ease tension" can easily appear crass or trite to the mourners. By "humor," I'm *not* suggesting that you take a Pearly Gates joke (of someone standing before Peter or Gabriel) then rewriting it with the deceased as the main character.

One solid rule about funeral humor? Never use jokes or canned humor.

There are few rules to guide you on funeral

humor, therefore exercise caution and compassion. The goal of a funeral is to comfort the mourners and share the compassion of Jesus. Obviously, never say anything that makes the deceased or the family appear stupid or ignorant. At my grandfather Atkins' funeral I understood my family and grandfather so well, that I knew what I could say.

"The heritage of Grandpa's family is sketchy at best. French-Canadian? Maybe. Grandpa did come from Kitchener, Ontario. When my family visited there a few years ago we found several 'Atkins' names in the phone book. Many years ago Aunt Maxine's grade-school teacher asked the students to investigate their family heritage. When Maxine asked her Dad about it he said, 'We're just a bunch of *Pine-Stump-Savages*.' She didn't know what that meant . . . .

"But now that we get you all together . . . Looking at you all, it's starting to become clear to me . . . ."

After Grandpa's funeral one lady said, "I see you have your Grandpa's sense of humor . . . ."

In retrospect I realized that the impromptu comment worked because it was something that my grandfather would have said. And more importantly, everyone knew it.

SUGGESTIONS FOR
SHARING HUMOROUS STORIES

At best using humor in a funeral is a judgment

call. To help you with that evaluation here are five guidelines with illustrations from several funerals.

When you appraise humorous accounts for a funeral consider: your knowledge of the family and deceased, the humorous stories that the family shared (in the interview), the funny tales the deceased told about him/herself, humorous accounts from *your* relationship with the deceased, and amusing reports from neighbors and friends of the deceased.

KNOWING THE FAMILY AND DECEASED

To a large degree selecting humor for a funeral is intuitive. Therefore the more familiar you are (or become) with the family the easier it is to know what details to share — especially when it comes to humorous accounts.

With some families humor would not be acceptable, like when the relationship with the deceased was a painful or bitter one. But for many people humor is a natural part of their lives. When I prepared my Grandfather Atkins' funeral message I could not avoid how his humor had effected our relationship with him.

Grandpa loved to visit people, especially family. And he usually arrived unannounced. I thought maybe it was a recent trait but I learned otherwise. My aunts and uncles said that when they were young Grandpa would load them into the car and drive to someone's home for a visit — without calling ahead.

And if they weren't home he would . . . .

I can tell from your laughter that he did that to you too.

If they weren't home he would move around some porch or lawn furniture, so that you would wonder, "Who did this?"

Some prankster or juvenile delinquent? No, just Grandpa again!

Grandpa and Vi would just drop in on you like you have "nothing else to do." I began to think that this trait was contagious when Uncle Bruce, Aunt Pauline, Dixie and Bill arrived at our doorstep one day . . . .

One night when we lived in Rolling Prairie, Indiana the phone rang at 3:00 A.M. It was Grandpa. He said that they were at the "Union" and wanted to know how to get to our house. At 3:00 A.M. the only 'Union' I could think of was the Carpenter's Union Hall — Grandpa was a retired union carpenter.

"In LaPorte or South Bend?" I asked.

"Neither," he replied. "We're at the Union 76 Station."

"Oh, just drive six miles East on Highway 20."

That was their first visit to Rolling Prairie. During his second visit we were building a new church so he pulled his trailer into the front yard to "inspect" the construction. We spent summer afternoons sipping iced tea while discussing the nuances between floor trusses and floor joists . . . .

His last unannounced visit came in June, 1988. When they stopped to see us there was no one home and no lawn furniture to move around . . . We were gone! Two days before that we had moved to Iowa!

HUMOROUS STORIES FROM THE FAMILY

To use humor you need not know the family as

well as you know your own. When minister Loran Miracle visited with Bernice Murphy's family before the funeral they shared how Bernice and her husband resolved their fights. When he became upset with her, he would go to the basement and play "I Wish I Was Single Again." When she got angry enough to confront him and he heard her coming down the stairs he would play, "Let Me Call You Sweetheart."

During the interview with the family, never seek out humorous stories. Wait for the family to volunteer them. Never ask, "Do you have any funny stories about your dad?" Sometimes I do ask for more details if a comment brings a chuckle from the family.

When I interviewed the Robert Perry family, his daughter from Idaho made a passing comment about squirt guns that brought a chuckle from Richard's wife, Betty. I asked about the squirt guns.

"While in Idaho," I said at the funeral, "Dick took Jeffery to the store and returned with the largest water gun that they could find — including extra 'water-clips.' When they came into the house Dick said to Jeffery's mom, 'I feel bad that I didn't get the rest of the kids something! What should I do?'

"She said, 'Well get each a squirt gun so that they can protect themselves!'

"So Dick went back to the store and bought each grandchild a water gun. But when he returned home he hung all of the guns on the wall and said (as grandfathers do), 'You cannot take these guns down until I *leave* for Michigan.'"

When my father-in-law's children shared about him they recalled these quotes of him.

"When one of the kids would fall down, Vic would say, 'Come over here and I'll help you up.' When the kids sang silly songs in the car, he would say, 'Can you guys sing, "Down the Street and Around the Corner."' When Tina would leave to go on a long trip, Vic would say, 'If you have any trouble . . . Write!'"

FUNNY TALES THE
DECEASED TOLD ABOUT HIM/HERSELF

One of the safest places to get funny stories about the deceased is from the tales they told about themselves. For example consider Katie Wild.

"Proverbs 31:25 — 'Strength and dignity are her clothing; she smiles at the future . . . ' Even while suffering with cancer, Katie never lost her perspective or her sense of humor. Rayford said that if he told Katie, 'The house is burning!' she would reply, 'Don't sweat the little stuff.' To Katie *things* were 'little stuff' and *people* were 'big stuff.'

"Katie's humor was shown one day when she and Pat Mogg were shopping in Traverse City, Michigan at a time when they both were dieting to lose weight. When they saw a candy store at the mall, Katie pointed at it and said to Pat, 'Let's go over there, at least we can *smell*.'

"Well, the store had free samples of 15 different kinds of candy — they tried them all.

"Pat asked Katie, 'Which one are we going to buy?' 'None,' Katie replied. 'We cannot eat that!'

Consider also Judy Phillips who told this account of "if the shoe fits . . . ."

"Judy's life illustrated that you reap what you sow. If you sow good, pleasant thoughts, you'll reap the benefit and joy of a positive attitude. It's what the Bible mentions when it says, 'Rejoice in the Lord always.' Judy often told stories about the silly things that she did. Once she was at church and her feet hurt. When she looked under the pew she found that she had two right shoes on — different colored shoes at that."

HUMOROUS ACCOUNTS FROM YOUR RELATIONSHIP WITH THE DECEASED

Occasionally you'll have humorous stories from your experiences with the deceased, like this one which shows the deceased's response to a funny situation.

"Dick Perry had taught his children, grandchildren, nieces, nephews and friend's children to snowmobile, water-ski, drive boats, salmon fish . . . .

"Dick enjoyed teaching young people and watching them face new challenges. But sometimes there were mishaps . . . .

"Dick taught many young people how to snow-mobile. Some of his latest *students* were my two sons. Up at Uncle Roy's cabin on Wolf Lake, we snowmobiled on the frozen lake as Dick began their lessons. 'Lean into the turns . . . ' he said. After some training and testing Dick decided they were ready for a short journey in the north woods of the Manistee National Forest along the Little Manistee River — that beautiful countryside that Dick enjoyed.

"My youngest son, Andrew, was only eleven on his first snowmobile driving experience. He did well until we came to a small trail with tight curves and huge oak trees. After he got a distance behind the others he hurried to catch up and took one sharp corner too quickly. Only then did he realize that snowmobiles don't climb three-foot diameter oak trees!

"Dick was patient and showed great restraint — maybe because a preacher was present.

"He showed less patience when that same son ran into one of two trees in an open, 40-acre field.

"My sons will always remember Dick for teaching them how to snowmobile and repairing the snow-mobiles afterward . . . ."

AMUSING REPORTS FROM
NEIGHBORS AND FRIENDS

Sometimes the funny anecdotes will come from people other than the family and the humor will depend on an embarrassing mistake or action of the deceased. In such cases either omit the account or ask the family if you should use it.

The day before Judy Phillips' funeral I visited Ben and Lois Graham, when Lois shared a humorous memory of Judy. Thinking it somewhat embarrassing, I asked Judy's daughter for permission before using it in the service.

"Judy and Bill often had Christian friends over after Sunday evening worship for a snack. One evening they invited Ben and Lois Graham to come with Lois' parents, Vanness and Laura Cook. Judy made pancakes for everyone, but she had a lot of trouble with them sticking to the griddle. Everyone agreed silently that 'these don't taste very good.' The next morning Judy realized she had used wallpaper paste for the pancake batter. That night, Judy's pancakes gave a whole new meaning to 'stick to your ribs.'"

HUMOR — USE WITH CAUTION!

Some people feel uncomfortable with humor at a "time for grieving." They think it is disrespectful to the deceased. Or, maybe their families always separated "business from pleasure."

During one family interview the daughter hinted at such a viewpoint and I even included a quote she had about her paternal grandfather who "was straight-laced and never mixed fun with business." She also mentioned that she wanted everyone to sit quietly before the service and that chatter before the funeral service disturbed her. Though I had known the family for years, I failed to perceive her sentiments.

During the same interview a brother of the deceased shared this amusing family memory. The family described Doris in three ways — by her love, her support and her listening ear.

Several family members said that she was always there when they needed her. Maybe Doris developed these traits in part, because she was the oldest of fourteen children. Doris' brother, Lester, gave us an inkling of what it may have been like with all those siblings — especially with so many brothers:

> Their grandfather Alwood owned a Whippet automobile which apparently didn't have much power. After Grandpa Alwood visited the family and went to leave, four of the boys — Charles, Wayne, Forest and Lester — would run out to the car and grab it by the back bumper. They didn't pick it up, they just held it. When Grandpa Alwood got out, they would scram. As soon as he got back into the car, they would grab the bumper again. This would continue, until their mom told them to quit teasing their Grandpa . . . .

As the audience laughed, I glanced at the daughter — she didn't even smile. I realized what I had done, but it was too late. Later I learned that she was not angry with me for telling the story.

Disappointed?

Maybe.

She was not upset about the information in the story. It was the principle (of sharing humor at a funeral) that disturbed her. *Any* humor would have displeased her.

I should have picked up on it in the interview. If I had realized the situation clearly, I would have omitted the story (which certainly was not *necessary* to the message) or at least asked her what she thought about me telling it.

One last bit of advice about funeral humor?

When in doubt, ask the family.

6

DEATH AND "THE WILL OF GOD"

One afternoon after our teen-aged paper boy, Darrold "Skeeter" Winters, delivered the papers in our neighborhood he dashed across an intersection on his bike and was struck by a truck. It was an unfortunate — and fatal — accident.

Skeeter's mom, dad and sister were shocked and grief stricken.

Because the Winters family had no church home, they had the Funeral Director, Louis Juday, ask me to speak at Skeeter's funeral. After we had agreed on the date and time Louis hesitated.

"One more thing, Kenn," Louis said. "The mother insists that her son wear a T-shirt in the casket. I tried to convince her otherwise but she insisted."

"Is it a special T-shirt?" I asked.

"Apparently, it was one of Skeeter's favorite shirts," Louis answered. "It has a picture of a donkey on a podium with its rear-end to the front. And it reads, 'When I die they will bury me faced down so you can kiss my _ _ _.'"

"Oh, I see . . . " I said.

"Kenn," Louis asked, "What can we do?"

"Will it be a closed casket service?"

"They want it open," Louis answered.

"Why put such a defiant shirt on him?" I asked. "I wonder if she is angry with God for 'taking her son.'"

"I think someone told her that Skeeter's death was 'the will of God' and that she should accept it because of that," Louis said.

That afternoon my visit with the Winters family confirmed that Skeeter's mom was bitter and angry with God for "taking her son from her."

Some well-meaning person had told her, "We don't understand it but it must fit into God's will. Skeeter's time was up. And God must have wanted him more than you do, so He took him."

Skeeter's mom questioned the character of a God who would snatch her teenaged son from her in such a violent way.

She wondered, "How could God be good and all-powerful and cause such suffering?"

Good question.

In this chapter we will discuss the illogical assumption that God has preset the death date for everyone. We'll consider God's providence, our personal freedom and suffering, especially as it relates to death, ministering to survivors and leading them beyond the bitterness that this misinformation causes.

THE CONFUSION ABOUT
DEATH AND GOD'S WILL

It surprises me how deep the confusion about the issue of death and the will of God runs among both the churched and unchurched. People utter statements like, "When your number is up; it's up!" "When God is ready for you, He'll call you home." The thought is that everyone has an personal clock counting down the time before he will exit this world.

This widespread presumption is expressed by songs like "Last Kiss," sung by Jay Frank Wilson. The song says that the girlfriend died in a car accident when they swerved to miss a stalled car on a rainy night.

Here's the chorus of this popular hit from 1961.

Where oh, where can my baby be?
The Lord took her away from me,
She's gone to heaven so I've got to be good,
So I can see my Baby, when I leave this world.

This number one song hit a double in theological bloopers. The worst error is that heaven can be earned by good works, "I've got to *be good* so I can see my baby when I leave this world." Trusting our works leads to death; trusting God's grace, Jesus' merit and His cleansing blood leads to life.

The song's second blunder teaches that "the Lord *took her* away . . . " If that statement is true it raises several questions. If it was God's will, did He *create* the accident to "take her"? Did He cause the other car to stall on the curve that rainy night? Or, do we deem it God's will because He did not stop the accident? Or, do we cry "God's will" because He did not miraculously rescue her from the fatal injuries?

How much of our lives does God program and control? Is He a puppeteer who pulls the strings and jerks us off stage? I question the assumption that no person leaves this world unless it's God's specific will and in His timing, place and manner.

What about the people who step out of God's will and use their freedom to defy God, such as those who commit suicide? Are they simply acting as agents of God's will? Certainly not.

How about murder victims? Are their deaths a part of God's will when murder specifically defies many commands of Scripture?

How about accidental deaths like Skeeter's? If an accident was the will of God — that is, His *intention* — then it is a designed event and is no longer an accident.

What about death by illness? Is our mismanagement of our health simply a predetermined Divine plan? What about the people who overeat, neglect their high blood pressure and die young from a heart attack? Is their death God's will or a result of their neglect of natural laws?

How can so many contradictory statements be sheltered equally under the umbrella of "God's will?"

Accepted blindly, the popular view that death is the predetermined will of God, leads us to confusion and bitterness rather than comfort.

If each specific death is the will of God, are we acting in rebellion against God if we save someone from death's clutches?

After a man's wife died the husband said to his minister Bob Palmer, "Well, I must just accept it. It's the will of God."

But as a doctor, he had been fighting for her life. He had called in the best specialists. He had used all the devices of modern science to fight disease. Was he fighting the will of God all that time? If she had recovered, would he have called her recovery the will of God? We cannot have it both ways. The woman's recovery and the woman's death cannot equally be the will of God in the sense of being His intention.

A mother weeping in anguish over the death of her baby said, "I suppose it's the will of God, but if only the doctor had come in time, he could have saved my baby." If the doctor had come in time, would he have been able to outwit the will of God?

Remember what the Scriptures said of Job after he suffered so much, including the death of all his children? "In all this Job did not sin, nor blame God" (Job 1:21 NASB). If God had "taken Job's children" the blame would squarely rest on God's shoulders.

GOD'S WILL AND OUR FREEDOM

Where does the providential will of God and the free choice of mankind meet when it comes to suffering and death?

Our good and omnipotent God granted us freedom in moral choices and natural choices — that is to employ natural objects. This freedom resulted in the abuse of the choices which brought suffering into the world. People suffer because of wrong moral choices, from abuse or neglect of natural laws, or because their lives are intertwined with millions of others who are abusing or neglecting moral and natural laws. To stop this suffering God would have to withhold freedom, because freedom implies the ability to choose between two alternatives — obedience and disobedience.

The following discussion is an overview of this theme as it applies to death, mourning and funerals. For a complete discussion of suffering read *A Loving God In A Suffering World*, by Jon Tal Murphree (InterVarsity Press, 1981).

THREE REASONS PEOPLE SUFFER

The reasons people suffer — and ultimately die — fit into three categories. People suffer because of unrighteousness; the abuse of God's moral laws. People suffer because of righteousness sake; the keeping of God's moral codes. People suffer because we live in a "dangerous world" where people effect one another through their abuse and neglect of moral or natural laws.

SUFFERING BECAUSE OF UNRIGHTEOUSNESS

> For what credit is there if you sin and are harshly treated, you endure it with patience?
>
> I Peter 2:20 (NASB)

Peter declares that Christian slaves gain no merit when they patiently endure harsh treatment from their masters after they rebel against God's moral law (such as stealing from their master). Peter directly connects their "harsh treatment" with their "sin" — their transgression of God's moral code.

> By no means let any of you suffer as a murderer, or thief, or evildoer, or a troublesome meddler;
>
> I Peter 4:15 (NASB)

Here Peter again connects suffering with disobedience to God's moral law. He mentions the suffering of murders, thieves, evildoers and meddlers without sighting an agent of wrath.

> For rulers hold no terror for those who do right, but for those who do wrong. Do you want to be free from fear of the one in authority? Then do what is right and he will commend you. For he is God's servant to do you good. But if you do wrong, be afraid, for he does not bear the sword for noth-

ing. He is God's servant, an agent of wrath to bring
punishment on the wrongdoer.

Romans 13:3,4 (NIV)

Paul refers to government as an agent of wrath,
who brings punishment on wrongdoers even unto
death. The Roman government used swords for
capital punishment, not for spankings.

In A Loving God In A Suffering World, Jon Tal
Murphree says:

> Rather than saying that suffering is penalty for
> sin, it would be more accurate to say that suffer-
> ing at times is the effect, the consequence, the
> automatic fallout of sin. The "punishment" is
> included in the scheme of things rather than being
> imposed directly on individuals. (Page 113.)

When God granted Adam and Eve the freedom
to choose, He granted them the ability to choose
between obedience and disobedience — to eat or
not to eat from the tree of the knowledge of good
and evil. If He had given them freedom to choose
but only one option, they would have had no freedom.

God's dilemma (speaking in human terms) was
to grant freedom and risk its abuses, or to withhold freedom, preventing its abuses and the suffering it creates. There is no such thing as freedom
without the ability to abuse freedom. Without it,
freedom is *not* freedom at all.

Murphree comments:

Without our freedom there might have been no

suffering as we know it, but neither could there have been sympathy. There would have been no hatred, but for the same reason there could have been no voluntary love. There would have been no sorrow, but neither could there have been comfort. There would have been no danger, but neither could there have been courage or heroism... Without moral freedom there would be no vice, but by the same token there could have been no virtue; virtue that is not freely chosen is no more than the "virtue" of fire to burn, water to freeze or light to shine. Mechanical robots programmed for certain behavior and deprived of freedom would have no privilege of fellowship with God. Both the very worst in life and the very best are made possible by moral freedom. Freedom itself precludes having the good without the possibility of the bad. (Page 41.)

Natural laws are neutral and can be manipulated equally well for evil or for good. We must have natural freedom to facilitate our moral freedom. For example, the laws of spontaneous combustion are used equally well by both the families keeping their homes warm and cooking their food, and the arsonist who destroys businesses and homes.

Moral freedom necessitates natural freedom to move and employ material objects. If we make a moral choice to help the hungry, but cannot manipulate the natural objects, we have no freedom. But the same is true if we make the *other* moral choice.

Some say that God could stop suffering by programming nature (or individuals) never to do evil. For instance, God could program automobiles to do good (taking children to school, shopping or the hospital) but not to do evil (robbing banks, kidnapping, or allowing drunk driving). But allowing freedom means risking the abuse of that freedom. That abuse — sin — is not desired by God, nor is it His will.

In Jesus' story of the Prodigal Son, the father gave the youngest son his share of the inheritance, so that he had the *freedom to choose*. The father — who models God in the story — gave his son the freedom (that the money created) and risked the son's abuse of that freedom.

A measure of evil and suffering exists because millions, even billions, of free people are choosing daily to use or abuse their moral freedom.

SUFFERING FOR RIGHTEOUSNESS' SAKE

But if you do what is right and suffer and patiently endure it, this finds favor with God.

I Peter 2:20 (NASB)

Blessed are those who are persecuted because of righteousness, for theirs is the kingdom of heaven. Blessed are you when people insult you, persecute you and falsely say all kinds of evil against you because of me. Rejoice and be glad, because great is your reward in heaven, for in the same way they persecuted the prophets who were before you.

Matthew 5:10-12 (NIV)

However, if you suffer as a Christian, do not be ashamed, but praise God that you bear that name.

I Peter 4:16 (NIV)

These three passages proclaim that people can suffer because of their good deeds. Jesus is the example.

Wasn't Jesus put to death for His good deeds? Yes, according to I Peter 2:18-25. Someone may ask, "Was not the death of Jesus the will of God?"

Yes it was. But consider the uniqueness of that situation. Jesus asked in the garden for the "cup of suffering" — His death — to pass from Him. But, He said, "Not My will but Yours be done." Death is a result of man's sin. Death was not God's intention, but He sent His Son to destroy the enemy called death, I Corinthians 15:26. To destroy death Jesus had to die and be raised victoriously over the grave. As Romans 8:28 says, God can turn "all things" including evil and suffering into "good." Jesus' death became our life, forgiveness and grace.

As a second example of suffering for goodness sake, consider Stephen who was stoned to death for proclaiming his faith in Jesus as the Messiah, Acts 7:54-60.

The author of Hebrews mentioned that "by faith . . . some escaped the edge of the sword" while others by that *same faith* "were slain by the sword," Hebrews 11:33,34,37.

Harlan Popov's book *Tortured For His Faith* describes the persecution of Christians under Bulgaria's former communist government. Sergei Kordakov's book *The Persecutor* shows his persecution of believers in the former U.S.S.R. and his conversion because of the faithfulness of the suffering

Christians he had beaten.

In part Christians suffer because they make correct moral choices and receive the backlash of the world's hatred for the truth.

SUFFERING BECAUSE WE LIVE IN A "DANGEROUS WORLD"

This category of suffering is the most difficult one to cope with emotionally, because it involves the suffering of innocent victims — victims of the evil actions of others. Victims of accidents because someone abused or neglected natural laws. Victims because our "dangerous world" is filled with disease and natural catastrophes, such as tornadoes, floods, lightning, and hurricanes. Jesus spoke of the death of *innocent* people because of evil actions of others and because of accidents.

> Now there were some present at that time who told Jesus about Galileans whose blood Pilate had mixed with their sacrifices. Jesus answered, "Do you think that these Galileans were worse sinners than all the other Galileans because they suffered this way? I tell you, no! But unless you repent, you too will all perish. Of those eighteen who died when the tower in Siloam fell on them — do you think they were more guilty than all the others who were living in Jerusalem? I tell you, no! But unless you repent, you too will all perish."
> Luke 13:1-5 (NIV)

Not all suffering is connected with a person's response to God's moral laws. Was the death of those Galileans God's will? No. In this case some

Galileans suffered because of the immoral actions of an unjust leader who abused his moral freedom and his governmental power.

The sins of one person can often effect innocent people around them; for extreme cases consider rape, incest and murder.

How can someone's death be God's will when the person who inflicted the fatal blow disobeys God's law in the process? A three-year-old girl rode her tiny tricycle in her front lawn one summer evening after dinner. A drunk driver screamed around the corner, lost control of his vehicle, raced through the yard then hit and killed the young girl. Trying to comfort the mother someone said, "It was God's will."

But how can it be God's will when no part of the equation was God's will? Was it God's will for the man to be drunk? Was it God's will for him to disobey the civil law about driving while intoxicated? Was it God's will for him to break the speed limit? Was it God's will for him to leave the safe traffic area, cross the lawn and hit a child riding her tricycle? "No" to all the above.

If the portions of the equation are not God's will then how can the sum total of the given parts become the will of God?

It cannot.

DEATH BY ACCIDENTS

At times, people suffer because *others* have neglected natural laws. Eighteen people from

Jerusalem were killed and their families mourned their loss, because the builders did not lay a proper foundation for the Tower of Siloam. Those eighteen died, not because God lined up the worst sinners from Jerusalem and dropped the Tower on them like some type of divine mouse trap. They died in an unfortunate accident, because they were in the wrong place at the right time. We live in a dangerous world.

Murphree suggests:

> Just as the abuse of moral freedom accounts for moral evil, the abuse of natural freedom accounts for a large measure of natural evil. Natural laws as well as moral laws can be broken. They may be inadvertently transgressed, but when they are broken something happens somewhere.
>
> For instance, a natural law says two objects cannot occupy the same space at the same time. When two approaching cars on separate streets arrive at the same intersection at the same time attempting to occupy the same space, something has to give. A natural law says an object that is unrestrained will move toward the earth. When the law of gravitation is transgressed, someone can get hurt. (Page 47.)

DEATH FROM DISEASE

In the same regard, much physical suffering, such as disease, results from neglect of natural laws.

After a man in India lost a child in a cholera epidemic he said, "Well, it's the will of God."

"Suppose someone crept up the steps onto your

veranda," the preacher said, "and deliberately put a wad of cotton soaked in cholera germ culture over your little girl's mouth. What would you think about that?"

"Who would do such a thing?" the Indian asked. "Such a person should be killed. What do you mean by suggesting such a thing?"

"Isn't that just what you have accused God of doing when you said it was His will? Call your child's death the result of mass ignorance, call it mass folly, call it mass sin. If you like, call it bad drains or communal carelessness, but don't call it the will of God."

Surely, we cannot identify as the will of God something for which a man would be put into jail, or a mental hospital.

GOD USES SUFFERING FOR GOOD

> As he (Jesus) went along, he saw a man blind from birth. His disciples asked him, "Rabbi, who sinned, this man or his parents, that he was born blind?"
> "Neither this man nor his parents sinned," said Jesus, "but this happened so that the work of God might be displayed in his life."
>
> John 9:1-3 (NIV)

God knew that this boy would be born blind and sought to use it to His glory. But to say that God can *make* something good out of what has happened, is different than saying God made suffering happen so that good may come about.

God does not cause the suffering that results from disease or genetics, but once it is present He wastes no time in using it for good, if we let Him. God does not desire suffering, does not cause it or purpose it, but He can *use* it and make good come from it.

A LOVING GOD CARES ABOUT THOSE WHO SUFFER

Eventually, healing came to Skeeter's family but it took time, love and teaching. Healing began when the grieving family experienced genuine compassion and love from Christians in the church. Seeing first the visible love of the church, they came to realize God's love and learned of God's will as well.

Certain circumstances call upon us to comment at the funeral on the issue of death and the will of God. Bruce Stoner's service was one.

Bruce was a 36-year-old man who was "as strong as a horse." He had a wife, two teen-aged daughters and a son in fifth grade. They had just bought 47 acres and a new home in March. One Tuesday evening the end of July, Bruce had an intense asthmatic attack. It was fatal.

Bruce's young widow not only grieved his loss, but blamed God for taking her husband, especially at a time when she and the children needed him most.

This death sent shock waves through the whole

community. Bruce was a popular and active member of the community. He was a member of the church, a volunteer firefighter, played on area softball teams, coached Pop Warner Football, coached Little League Baseball, and delivered fuel for the LaPorte County Co-Op.

The greeting line for viewing of the deceased ran the whole length of the funeral home and out into the street. Over a thousand people visited with the family that day.

My ties with the family had remained close even though I had left that congregation four years before.

When Bruce's mom called with the news, I told them I would drive to Indiana from Michigan to be with the family for the viewing and funeral. Whether or not I spoke at the funeral was not as important as being with the family. Bruce's parents, Les and Lois, had lost another son, Mark, years before and I knew how *that* loss still brought tears to their eyes.

When the family asked me to participate in the service, I struggled with what to say. I knew Brenda and others were asking, "Why did God take Bruce?" The issues were too involved to articulate every aspect, and the philosophical jargon seemed inappropriate for a funeral setting. I prayed for wisdom.

After the local minister opened with Scripture and prayer, "The Old Rugged Cross" was played at the largest funeral I had ever seen. I began the personal profile with the list of survivors, then

spoke of Bruce's three primary characteristics —
he was an Encourager, a Competitor and a Friend.
I illustrated each with stories and anecdotes about
his wife, children, Christian friends, and told of
the basketball and softball games we had played
together.

I then addressed the issue of Bruce's *untimely*
death in this way:

Situations like today are a tragedy — a young
man leaves behind a young family. Certainly not
intentional on his behalf nor anyone's. But it's
tragic not only because we lose a husband, son,
dad, brother and friend, we also lose memories . . .
Future memories that were yet to unfold. We
think, "Well, what would it have been like, if he
were still here?"

There will certainly be occasions in the future
when you will think, "Oh, I have to tell Bruce
about that." And then you'll pause and think, "No,
I cannot. He's gone."

This occasion warns us, friends, that you're not
promised tomorrow and neither am I. If you have
something you want to say to someone, say it
today. Tell them. Love them. Have a bridge to
build? Don't wait until tomorrow. You're not
promised tomorrow.

Bruce spent his life, not on the sidelines spectat-
ing, but on the field participating, as if he knew
this might be the last game . . . .

On a difficult day like today we ask ourselves,
"Why? Why, did this happen?"

We know the medical reasons why but we ask,
"Why?" seeking a purpose to this event. Some
people may erroneously say to the family, "Be
comforted because this death must be the will of
God." I want you to know that death is not the will
of God. God is not a puppeteer in heaven with

strings on all our earthly lives, who deciding our time is up, pulls on the strings jerking us out of this life into the next.

God is not such a God.

The God the Bible describes and the Father of Jesus, is a God who loves you so much He gives you freedom to love Him because you choose to. Everything that happens in our lives is an interaction of our free choices and those of others. God has not appointed a specific time and moment for each person to leave this life. If He were such a God, I would have trouble with that presumption when someone is murdered. I would ask what kind of God would condone that kind of death, when even in His Word He says, "Thou shall not murder."

So we have to be careful about simply, glibly covering everything by saying, "This is the will of God." Death is not the will of God. It was never the will of God for death. You remember the story of Adam and Eve in the Garden, don't you? There was a tree of knowledge of good and evil and God wanted life for His creation. But He said that the day you eat of that tree — the day you disobey Me with your freedom to choose — you shall surely die. The decay which lead to physical death began on the day they ate.

It was not a part of God's will for death; God's plan for us is life. God is not simply snatching people away from us, He wants to love us and show us His direction.

As a matter of fact, God loves us so much He gave us the freedom to reject Him or blame Him for the suffering we endure, because we think Him unloving or unpowerful. Think of the story of the Prodigal Son. The reason the father gave the younger son his inheritance (before the father died) was to give the son the freedom (that the money provided) to choose the father's will or to reject it. The son chose to run off to a foreign land, but later he "came to his senses" and returned. When the father saw him on the horizon, he ran to his son, embraced him and welcomed him home.

The father did not cause the suffering that the son endured, but when the son turned to the father for comfort, he received more comfort than he could have ever dreamed . . . .

7

TOUGH FUNERALS AND FUNERALS FOR TOUGH PEOPLE

Funerals are a time to remember the deceased, and to say good-bye. The most comforting message includes personal details of the deceased. But what can we do in situations where their is little personal details about the deceased, such as in the death of an infant? Or, how do we handle the personal profile of a mentally handicapped person? Or a suicide victim? What can we say about a deceased who was a bitter, abusive parent, who left wounded people in his wake? What can we say that is both honest, yet will comfort the family?

In the first section of this chapter we will discuss and illustrate how to deal with *tough funeral* settings: violent deaths, infants, children, suicides, and the mentally handicapped.

In the second section we will discuss funeral setting for *tough people*, such as bitter, abusive parents and unrepentant reprobates.

HANDLING TOUGH FUNERALS

Scott Taube was Angela Shufflebeam's minister when she was murdered. His suggestions for supporting a family in the first days of grief and shock apply in general to the situations of infant deaths, fatal accidents of youths and suicides.

FUNERALS FOR VICTIMS OF VIOLENT DEATHS

Angela Shufflebeam was a fifteen-year-old sophomore who was involved in her church youth group (leading many of her friends to Christ), future teacher's program, on the honor roll, on the tennis team, wrote for the school newspaper, and was selected as "Student of the Week" a few days before her death. Angela was bright and cheerful. Her short life had already touched so many. After school on April 18th, Angela was assaulted in her home and murdered by a fifteen-year-old boy.

When Scott Taube was alerted by the family to the crisis, he and his wife went directly to Angela's family to provide support. It was not easy. Scott, who presided at her funeral, was with the family during the first hours and days after the tragedy.

From his experience of that agonizing time, Scott offered these suggestions about supporting a shocked, grieving family.

• *Be yourself.* Scott and his family opened their home to Ken and Karen Martin (Angela's mother and stepfather) the evening of the murder and stood beside them as they called their families to relay the awful news. Scott said, "We said very little. We touched them, hugged them and consoled with words from our aching hearts."

• *Live out the compassion of Scripture.* Don't just quote it. Scott said, "We didn't say very much. We did not even bring up the written Word, we became the Word in action. Nothing soothes the heart more than a genuine Christlikeness."

• *Be sensitive to the family's need for privacy.* Don't be afraid to ask if they would like to be alone. "My wife and I became the clearing center for all the Martin's messages that came from all over the city and all over the country," Scott said. "We took messages and relayed them at the appropriate time. We also helped to protect them from the press — at their own request."

• *Be aware of and sensitive to "well-meaning" people.* Many people want to do something to help. Others are just curious. "It amazed me how many people just want to check out the family and the events that surround such a crime," Scott said. "We assisted in the funeral arrangements and preparations only as much as they desired." Involvement in the arrangements can begin the healing process for the family.

• *Pray privately in your prayer closet for the family and for your role as a minister.* Ask for God's wisdom as you prepare your remarks at the funeral service.

Scott Taube began Angela's funeral message by speaking of her Christian faith and her assurance of heaven. Then five of Angela's friends shared their thoughts about her. Afterward Scott quoted one of Angela's poems he said:

"Smiling, loving, laughing, living for today was Angela's way. And with such a life, such vitality and vibrancy, and so much to live for our hearts cry out with one question. 'Why? Why her? Why now?'

"The answer? Satan.

"Only one as evil as he could provoke a person to commit such a crime. And while Satan may call himself a victor in this tragedy, he is ultimately the loser.

"Angela is the victor. Angela is very much alive. If she is permitted to share with us today as she stands happy with our Lord Jesus . . . ."

Later, again speaking of her faith Scott said:

"On one occasion Angela came into my office crying. When I asked her what was wrong, she said that she wanted to know how she could do more for Jesus and how she could get closer to Him. Never had a young person in my ministry expressed such great love for the Lord. Oh, how Angela wants all of you to have the very salvation and joy in Christ that she is experiencing even during our time of grieving over her loss . . . ."

Scott read a tribute to Angela which was written by her relatives and closed with one of Angela's poems entitled, "The Cry," which ended, "These are the words I give. Please be smart, and brave and remember to forgive."

FUNERALS FOR INFANTS AND CHILDREN

Elderly people are supposed to die; children are not. It is something unexpected when a child dies, yet they do, of course. According to the National Center for Health Statistics, approximately 94,000 young people between infancy and age 24 die every year. The leading causes for their deaths include: cancer, homicides, suicide, crib death (SIDS), and accidents such as drowning and car crashes.

The statistics fail to capture the shock, grief and despair that a couple feels when they lose a child or baby. Their grief is the most intense I have ever shared. The death of a child has a permanent effect on the parents. I have seen some couples who could not cope with their grief together, get a divorce. Maybe other circumstances were at work in their marriages but their different responses to grieving for their child pushed them apart.

Other couples depend upon God for their comfort and grow closer to Him and each other. The two best elders that I have ever served with were men with broken hearts. Each had lost a child to disease. Their brokenness lasted a lifetime. When a sermon or hymn reminded them of their children, tears would trickle down the cheeks of these strong, successful men. God took their brokenness and made the weak strong. He bound up the brokenhearted and they, in turn comforted others. And God was honored.

When Brock Neff died from crib death, SIDS — Sudden Infant Death Syndrome, I shared these words in his memory.

> Frank Deford wrote, "Elderly people die with achievements and memories. Children die with opportunities and dreams."
>
> Facing death is never easy for any of us, but to have a child die is something almost too tragic to comprehend.
>
> Brock's short life touched all of us here. Yet finding words to express ourselves is not easy, because our love for him and with him is bound up in feelings, emotions, and actions — actions we will miss. There will be times we will expect him to be there when we turn and yet he won't come.
>
> In those times, don't give up, don't give in, give it all to Him.
>
> Losing Brock is difficult because he had so much in front of him. This adds to our loss. Just this last month he had begun to talk. He called his mother "Ma Ma," his father "Da Da," his grandparents "Pa Pa," the Boston Terrier "Sally" (which to him meant any dog), and Brock called Aaron, his sister, "Ernie."
>
> Brock had just learned to swing, enjoy playing with balls and marbles, and to get candy from grandma's candy dish. Last week he had learned how to sneak over to the neighbor's, when he and Aaron were outside.
>
> Aaron and Brock were close and she treated him like a mother would . . . .

144

We all loved Brock and he loved us all . . . .

In times like these we are tempted to give up on life and give in to bitterness. Instead let's give it all — the pain and suffering — to God.

Don't Give Up On Life: (Read — John 14:1-6.)

Brock's death was not the will of God. God did not snatch him from us . . . .

God did provide a remedy for death and the separation it causes. The Bible often replaces the word death with the word *sleeping* . . . (See comments on *Sleeping* from Chapter 4.)

Don't Give In To Bitterness And Anger.

If Brock's death was the planned intention of God, we would have every reason to question the character of God. If God did will this, then we should be angry and bitter. But God did not will this . . . (See comments about God's will in Bruce Stoner's service in Chapter 6.)

In this world there is only one guarantee. That is that Jesus Christ is the victor through His bodily resurrection. He is the only one who can offer hope to see Brock again and comfort to our hearts and minds today.

Give All Your Pain And Grief To God.

I cannot say that I understand how you feel just now. But I know how much it hurts me and that your pain must be even more intense. I'm not going to be presumptuous and say that I understand your grief — I don't.

But I know Someone Who has lost His Son. He understands what it means to lose an only son. God loves you so much that He gave His only Son, so that on days like today your despair could be turned to hope . . . .

During the armed conflict in the Far East a couple had their only son stationed in Korea. Because he was there, they went to the library and read all about that region and kept up with the news in the daily papers. They had a vested interest in the activities there. Now you have a child stationed in Heaven. Go to church and share with people who are journeying there. Read your Bibles to learn the route there and to hear the news of Heaven. Study about it and prepare yourself in the grace of God to journey there . . . You have a vested interest there . . . .

Brock's Personal Profile included some details about his young life; unfortunately with younger babies, you don't even have those details. For these babies Minister Tim Sipes uses this three point outline:

What This Death Means To The Child?
· Gone into Heaven
· Will not suffer the pain of this world

What Does This Death Mean To Us?
· Grieving
· Loss of future dreams
· Disappointment

This Death Means A Renewed Interest In Heaven.
· Heaven is a real place
· The path to Heaven

FUNERALS FOR SUICIDE VICTIMS

Suicide creates the most difficult loss for a family to bear. After a suicide every relationship is irreparably shattered and grief is compounded by guilt.

According to the World Health Organization an estimated one thousand people commit suicide every day.

In the United States, more people die from suicide than murder and there are more suicides than drownings. Only traffic accidents rank higher as to violent deaths — some experts claim that many single-person accidents are auto-suicides.

On the average someone in the United States attempts suicide every minute, and sixty to seventy of them succeed each day.

Suicide victims cover almost every conceivable range — even as young as 8 years old. Suicide claims lives of men and women, every race and religion, from the poor to the very wealthy. Suicide knows no prejudice.

Of the six suicides mentioned in the Bible five were committed by people in battle situations where death or dishonor were their only options: Saul and his armor-bearer (I Sam. 31:4-6), Ahithophel (II Sam. 17:23), Zimri (I Kings 16:18,19), and Samson (Judg. 16:30). The only non-warrior to commit suicide was Judas Iscariot (Matt. 27:3-5).

There were however, some people in non-military settings, who out of despair wished to die: Job (Job 3:11, 38:4, 40:8), Elijah (I Kings 19:1-18), Jonah (Jonah 4:1-4), and the Philippian Jailer (Acts 16:27,28).

Curiously, Elijah's story serves as a model for helping someone overcome depression: food from the ravens (supplying for physical needs), words of comfort and encouragement (from God's Word), and a new person to share the burden (Elisha).

The Philippian Jailer literally found salvation in the comforting words of Paul and Silas. (Acts 16:25-34.)

In "Wounds That Won't Heal" Sylvia Root Tester challenges us to empathize with the victim. She wrote:

> Sadness heals; depression gets stuck. Think about your worst sorrow. The worst emotional pain you ever felt. And think of it lasting and lasting, no matter how you try or what you do, not week or months, but for years and years. Think of how tired you would become, how distraught, how illogical perhaps, and certainly how desperate for relief. With that in mind . . . We can better understand how a person might consider suicide.
>
> (The *Lookout*, February 6, 1983, Page 4.)

A. Alvarez, an English poet who early in his adult life attempted suicide, wrote a powerful and hopeful book about overcoming suicide called *The Savage God*. In it he says, "A suicidal depression is a kind of spiritual winter, frozen, sterile, unmoving."

In "Suicide . . . Helping Survivors Survive" grief therapist Victor Parachin wrote,

> A death by suicide triggers great amounts of anger and guilt. But some of those feelings can be balanced by struggling to see that suicide is not usually so much a deliberate, hostile act as a gesture of utter hopelessness and despair. Reminders that the person was so driven by emotional whirlwinds that it was impossible to sense any ray of hope can temper the emotional impact of a sui-

cide.

One of the best responses to a suicide I ever heard, came through a sermon delivered by the minister of a young man who shot himself. With great eloquence, this preacher was able to convey tremendous hope:

"Our friend died on his own battlefield. He was killed in action fighting a civil war. He fought against adversaries that were as real to him as his casket is real to us. They were powerful adversaries. They took toll of his energies and endurance. They exhausted the last vestiges of his courage and his strength. At last these adversaries overwhelmed him. Only God knows what this child of His suffered in silent skirmishes that took place in his soul."

(The *Lookout*, May 3, 1992, Page 7.)

FUNERALS FOR
MENTALLY HANDICAPPED PEOPLE

Presenting a personal profile for a mentally handicapped person raises many questions. How do we deal with his handicap? What Biblical affirmation applies to his life? What value does God place on a handicapped person? What about the issue of heaven and salvation? Can I suggest that the deceased is "with the Lord"?

Paul wrote in I Corinthians 12:22-24:

On the contrary, it is much truer that the members of the body which seem to be weaker are necessary; and those members of the body, which we deem less honorable, on these we bestow more abundant honor, and our unseemly members come to have more abundant seemliness, whereas

our seemly members have no need of it. But God
has so composed the body, giving more abundant
honor to the member which lacked (NASB).

Speaking of the church, Paul affirms the value
of each — even seemingly *lowly* — member of the
body. I believe that this *principle* of "giving more
honor to the members that lack" applies to the
value of every person, especially the mentally
handicapped. God specializes in taking the weak
and shaming the strong. Within His grace, God
compensates their weakness with other strengths.
Idiot savants illustrate this principle.

Idiot savants are severely mentally handicapped
people with some incredible skill. Some can replay
any song after the first time they hear it. Some
memorize *anything* they read and can answer any
questions concerning the facts therein. Others can
sing . . . The list goes on and on. Curiously, the
word "savant" is a synonym for philosopher, sage
and scholar. I realize these are extreme examples,
but I have found that same specialness in "ordi-
nary" mentally handicapped people that I have
known. They have never been asked to be on
national talk shows, but they have touched many
lives with their unique traits.

When it comes to the issue of salvation, I treat a
mentally handicapped person just as I would a
child who never reached the age of accountability.
Though physically they may reach a very old age,
mentally handicapped people never reach "the
mental age of accountability."

One such person was Ralph Douglas Harris. Everyone knew him as Doug. I ended Doug's short personal profile with these comments, then addressed the issues of God's value for mentally handicapped people in general and Doug in particular.

"Doug enjoyed fishing and other outdoor activities but most of all, it seemed, he was a die-hard Chicago Cub Fan. A Cub fan is a *real* fan indeed.

"Personally, I enjoyed being around Doug. He struck me as shy but happy person with a lot of love to give to others.

"Handicapped people have a special place in my heart. More importantly, they have a special place in God's heart. When I was younger I questioned, 'Why does God *cause* people to be handicapped?'

"The answer is: God does not cause handicaps. Suffering is a result of mankind's rebellion against God with the freedom of choice He gave us. When Adam and Eve (and the rest of us really) rebelled against God, four basic relationships were broken: Man and God, Man and himself, Man and other men, and Man and nature. Part of the result was disease, and mental and physical handicaps. Handicaps are not the specific result of the sin of the parents or child, but are a consequence of society's rebellion against God and His natural and moral laws.

"Though God does not cause physical or mental handicaps, He does know if someone will be handicapped and compensates for that in other areas of their lives. To God, we are all valuable.

"God has created you with talents and abilities which make you a useful and valuable person in society and His church. You have the freedom to use your talents for God or against Him. But the handicapped person has just as special a purpose in life as you do. Doug Harris was, in a sense, on a mission from God. God had a purpose for Doug's life that we as his family and friends may not now know — one day it will be revealed.

"An unknown author wrote this poem, 'Heaven's Very Special Child.'

> A meeting was held quite far from earth:
> It's time again for another birth,
> Said the angels to the Lord above.
> This child will need much love.
> His progress may seem very slow.
> Accomplishments he may not show
> And he'll require extra care
> From the folks he meets way down there.
> He may not run or laugh or play;
> His thoughts may seem quite far away.
> In many ways he won't adapt,
> And he'll be known as handicapped.
> So let's be careful where he's sent,
> We want his life to be content.
> Please, Lord, find parents who
> Will do a special job for you.
> They will not realize right away
> The leading role they're asked to play,
> But with this child sent from above
> Comes stronger faith and richer love.
> And soon they'll know the privilege given.
> In caring for this gift from Heaven.
> Their precious charge, so meek and mild,
> Is Heaven's very special child."
> (Anonymous)

"Doug is with Jesus now; so let's not grieve on his behalf, but for ours. It's because of our love, and our emptiness that we grieve.

"Doug is not only with God, but he is now whole and complete — all the struggles and handicaps are gone. Doug is perfect beyond compare, as is everyone who enters Heaven.

"Christian biologist John Clayton wrote about that assurance:

"'Some years ago, I noticed a tombstone in a cemetery in Tomah, Wisconsin. It said:

Here lies Sarah Burknett
Born blind April 4, 1911
Sight restored
August 14, 1964

"'The victim of mankind's free moral choice badly made, Sarah Burknett suffered a great deal perhaps for all her 53 years. If she died a Christian, she will experience forever a condition so marvelous that her lack of physical sight will be barely remembered. Truly, it is great to be alive and a child of an Almighty and all wise God.'"

[*Does God Exist?*, March-April, 1983, page 11]

FUNERALS FOR TOUGH PEOPLE

How can we share personal details about a deceased who was cruel, abusive or bitter? What should we say when the family expresses a sense of relief, even elation that he died?

What if he was a bitter person who was spiteful to those closest to him? What if he was an abusive father? What if the deceased was a reprobate who shunned his family?

These messages I call "funerals for tough people." They provide their own set of problems, both for the family struggling to cope with irreparable relationships, and for the minister asked to speak at the funeral service.

Frankly, I have been tempted to "put all the cards on the table" and, rather tactlessly, proclaim that the deceased was "a moron." Like someone said, "Everyone has a purpose in life, even if it's only to serve as a bad example." I realize, however, that the family *already* knows what kind of person he (or she) was. My goals are to provide a Biblical perspective on their loss, share God's comfort and lead them to Christ. Funerals, after all, are for the living, not the dead.

Refusing to acknowledge that there was strife within the relationships won't minister to the family's'needs either. I realized this clearly after I presided for the funeral of a man, who apparently had been a complete reprobate. I had sensed that from a few side comments of his sister but I did not pursue the theme. I had visited the young man several times while he was in a nursing home before his death.

At his funeral I spoke of my impression of him, from the my visits with him. My comments were brief but kind, even hopeful. I believe people can change through God's grace. But I knew something lurked deeper beneath the surface when his sister said to me a couple of times after the funeral, "That wasn't *my* brother you were talking about. That's okay though, you didn't *really* know him."

I followed up on that family but she was never willing to talk about these issues.

FUNERALS FOR BITTER/UNLOVING PEOPLE

How can we share personal details about the deceased and yet remain honest and comforting? The most meaningful messages shared under these circumstances come from ministers who can identify in some way with the family's pain. Their testimony of how God healed their broken heart — even if the relationships were never healed — can comfort the grieving family.

Steve, my minister friend from Illinois, was called upon to do the funeral of "John Jenson."

Steve's father was an alcoholic which created a lot of turmoil for Steve in his youth. Though Steve and his father talked about "things," he had always wanted to have a *real* conversation with his father about anything with *value*, not if whether the Chicago Bears and Chicago Cubs won or lost. Though Steve never obtained that relationship with his dad, he learned that his Heavenly Father did affirm him, love him and desired a close relationship with him. Steve had dealt with the pain and it was healed by his relationship with God. This closure allows him to guide others to that same healing and peace.

Because of Steve's experiences with his dad (and the healing of his Heavenly Father), Steve understood some of the emotions, regrets, and pain the Jenson family felt.

John Jenson manipulated others, abused alcohol, and weighed over 500 pounds. When he died he was laid to rest in an extra-wide, reinforced casket. To lower it into the ground required two grave plots and a forklift. Months before, Steve found indications that John had abused his stepchildren. John told lots of stories about things he had done as an airline pilot, undercover narcotics informant, motorcycle gang member . . . No one, not even his second wife, knew what to believe. He blew a lot of smoke, thinking himself a smooth talker and a powerfully persuasive speaker. John knew he could talk himself out of any jam.

For the personal profile Steve decided to share some of his personal testimony concerning his struggle with his own father and the healing he found in the Heavenly Father. Here are some excerpts from Steve's message for John Jenson:

> From the family I have learned . . . That John was born in Hanover, Illinois in 1932. He spent much of his boyhood growing up with his grandparents near the Savanna, Illinois area. Before he was out of school he moved to the Chicago area. After high school he held a job as a mechanic or a maintenance man for Northwest Airlines — though John dreamed of being a airline pilot — that dream never came true.
>
> Years later John opened a motorcycle shop, then started Mobile Mechanics — a van filled with a

"First Aide Kit" (auto parts, batteries . . .) for cars. It was like a traveling auto parts store with its own mechanic. Still later, he tinkered with buying and selling antiques . . . .

Honestly, I have struggled with how to characterize the life of John Jenson. How do you characterize a character? For all things that John was and was not, he was an interesting person — as well as a challenge.

Sometimes people play out their whole lives trying to be what they think others want them to be. People often think of themselves only as the different roles they play, such as a father, worker, mechanic, salesman, fisherman . . . Sometimes people play so many roles that they become a facade and we really don't know who they are. They don't know either. Their roles are like the skins of an onion; when you strip them all away, there's nothing left. It was all skins and no core.

Sadly, some people are that way and even sadder is the fact that they often leave a trail of wounded friends and relatives in their wake.

When such a person happens to be your father it makes life difficult. Charles Cooley in his sociological study, "The Looking Glass Concept of Self" says that we view ourselves the same way the most important person in our lives sees us. A "most important person" in each of our lives is our father. How our father thinks of us and treats us affects how we feel about ourselves for a lifetime. No father is perfect and some relationships with fathers can be rather painful.

I know what I'm talking about. People commonly think that ministers come from "perfect homes." Such is rarely the case. I have hurts of my own with my father. He is an alcoholic and it pains me even today that I cannot have a real conversation with my dad. I love my dad, more now than ever, but I still regret that I cannot converse with him. I never remember him telling me he loved me until I was seventeen and he woke me in the middle of the night after he had come home from the tavern. He was drunk and the next morning he didn't remember a word he had said. I understand the pain, the regret . . . .

But I also understand healing and love. The affirmation I never received from my dad while I was growing up, I now receive from my Heavenly Father and from my big Brother Jesus Christ. God has healed the brokenness of my heart and filled me with love — especially for my dad. That healing is available through Jesus . . . .

Steve then shared a message about our hope in the resurrection of Jesus. Therein he warned that, "Jesus in the only way. No one will be able to 'blow smoke' at God during the judgment. No one will get in by convincing God of anything, no matter how smooth they talk or how persuasive they speak . . . .

FUNERAL FOR A DRUNKEN REPROBATE

Because Steve had shared the testimony of his pain and how God healed his anguish, Tressa asked him to preside over her son's funeral. Tressa's father was an alcoholic and her son, Don, had lived for the bottle. Her grief was compounded by the irreparable relationship. Don had occasionally held a job, to get money to drink. He lived only 4 miles from his mother but rarely called her. He had not seen his two (now high-school aged) children for several years. One day Don passed his daughter on the street and he did not even recognize her.

At the time of Don's death, someone counseled Tressa to call a minister friend who had worked with Don. She told Steve, "Someone suggested that I call Ray and have him do the funeral. I decided not to. I love Ray, but you are my comfort."

That was Tressa's way of articulating that she knew that Steve *understood* the pain she had with her dad and son, because he had dealt with similar pain with his dad and brother.

Steve used the world events surrounding Don's birth as a metaphor for the struggles of Don's life.

Don was born in Vernon Township on July 7th, 1944 — 47-years ago. Three months after his birth his dad, Levi, left for Europe to fight in World War II.

When Levi departed for military service, he left behind three little boys and his wife. God answered many prayers and brought him back safely to his young family, then Tressa's daughter and youngest son were born.

Don was artistically inclined . . . .

Don was born when the world was at war — in a tremendous struggle. Germany, France, Netherlands, England, Egypt, Italy, Russia, China, Japan and the United States all struggled in a battle for "right" and freedom.

Some people, like the world in 1944, spend their whole lives struggling and the reasons they struggle are often unclear. Some people rise above those struggles to succeed . . . Others do not. There are no pat answers. We are left to wonder, "Why?"

If you'll pardon the personal comments, I'd like to

share that I've my struggles too. People think that ministers come from perfect homes. Many do not. My father is an alcoholic and I have a younger brother who today struggles against narcotics and alcohol. My younger brother was even numbered with the homeless in America. I love my dad. I love my brother. My heart breaks for them. I want to have a normal, loving relationship with them, but I cannot. I know the struggles, the pain and the storms that come and God is the only One who can calm the storm. From the story of Mark 4:35-41, we learn that Jesus sometimes calms the storm and sometimes He calms His child . . . .

AN HONEST LOOK INSIDE

How can we comfort families in these situations when we do not have experiences like Steve's to draw from? For me, it is a matter of looking deeply and honestly into my own heart and finding the pain that I often leave concealed. Our experiences may not be as dramatic as Steve's, but they are just as valid when it comes to illustrating how God can heal a broken heart.

Sharing this type of testimony, whether in a private counseling or a public message, must not be an outpouring of unresolved pain. Before we can share it we must experience a healing closure, so we can see past the pain and share hope. Note the love Steve expressed towards his dad and his desire for a relationship with him. You sense no bitterness toward his dad, only love mixed with some regret.

So, will we remain safely concealed or will we open up and share our personal testimonies? Are we willing to leave our security and allow God to comfort others through the comfort He has given us?

"Blessed be the . . . God of all comfort; who comforts us in all our affliction so that we may be able to comfort those who are in any affliction with the comfort with which we ourselves are comforted by God." (II Cor. 1:3,4 NASB)

8

FUNERAL FOLLOW UP:
Mourning and Ministry Don't End at the Graveside

In the weeks and months that follow a death, the grieving process continues, but the overwhelming flood of encouragement that swept in for the funeral slows to a trickle.

A house once full of relatives becomes a collection of silent rooms. Sympathy cards no longer arrive with the morning mail. The grieving friends and relatives return to work and daily schedules, but the pain continues though it is easier to control the tears. Months and even years later, grief surfaces when a survivor encounters the deceased's favorite flower, food, song or hymn. Special days — birthdays, Christmas, anniversaries, Memorial Day, Mother's Day — are often moments of renewed loss and mourning.

Mourning does not end at the committal service, but far too often ministry does.

In *The Minister as Crisis Counselor*, David K. Switzer wrote:

> In a pilot study, one community service took the initiative in contacting 20 bereaved families, eight days after the death of a family member, to offer their counseling services. The stated assumption of the agency was that the persons' usual sources of support would be inadequate at this particular time. The fact that 18 of the 20 families accepted the offer is probably some kind of judgment upon the ministry of the area. (Page 147.)

Fortunately, there are ways that ministers can follow up on the families after a loss. More importantly, we can encourage and train Christians for this comforting ministry.

The ministry of Christians comforted Marjorie Gordon, after the accidental death of her 25-year-old son, David. She wrote, "The days, weeks, and months that followed were bearable only because many friends touched us with their care, love, and prayers. We were like the little boy who was afraid of the dark. When he was left alone in his bedroom, he said, 'I know God is here, but I need someone with skin on.'"

As we will see, this comforting ministry is easier than it may seem. The chief qualification? Concern.

Sometimes it is other Christians, not the minister, who can best comfort those who mourn.

Karen's seventeen-year-old son, Joey, died in an auto accident when his friend swerved to miss a deer and struck a bridge abutment. At the public viewing, Karen sat stoic. Many people tried to comfort her with words and hugs. They said, "We're really sorry." "Is there anything we can do?" Some even said, "We understand what you're going through."

Karen did not cry. She knew they did not understand.

Later, Karen's neighbor, Annette, came into the viewing room. When their eyes met, Karen stood up for the first time. They embraced, neither spoke. They sat and cried.

Karen had received many hugs that day, but this was a hug of identity. Karen knew, without a word, that Annette understood her pain — Annette had lost her son to cancer seven months earlier.

I never understood many of the aspects of grief until I lost my father-in-law, Vic Bierschbach. He was more than a father-in-law; he was my friend. We traveled on many fishing trips together. He taught me fly-fishing, gave me my first fly-rod and was a subject of my magazine articles on the topic. Losing him allowed me — rather reluctantly — to "sit where the people sit." Now, when others lose a parent I can better understand. In their eyes I can see my own pain.

REASONS TO FOLLOW UP

There are two main reasons to keep in contact

with the survivors: mourning does not end at the graveside and seeds of the Gospel, planted during the service, need cultivating.

Grief and mourning do not end at the funeral.

Recent studies attest that some of the oldest funeral traditions may be the wisest. One such tradition was that a widow could wear black for a whole year after her husband's death. This visible sign reminded everyone that her grief did not end in six weeks.

In his book David Switzer commented on a study entitled, "The First Year of Bereavement," written by C. Murray Parkes (*Psychiatry*, 33, November 1970). About the duration of the grieving process, he wrote:

> A summary of the situation after thirteen months showed loneliness still to be a very common problem. Social adjustment was rated by the interviewer as good in five instances, fair in nine, poor in eight. Six widows had definitely worse health than before the death of their husbands, and none was healthier. Six reported themselves as happy, seven as sad, two as neutral, and seven as having moods that fluctuated between happiness and sadness. In terms of overall adjustment, the interviewer made the judgment that three were very poorly adjusted, depressed, and grieving a great deal, nine were intermittently disturbed and depressed, six showed a tenuous adjustment which might be easily upset, and four had made a good adjustment. The conclusion is that even after thirteen months, the process of grieving was still going on, and although all the principle features were past their peak, there was no sense in which grief could be said to have finished. (Page 154.)

Often the *firsts* of that year, like his birthday, their anniversary, and holidays, become intense days of mourning. Katie and Rayford Wild shared many activities together. Each December they traveled to the Department of Natural Resources' check station for opening day of elk season. After her death, he asked me to go with him that December. Knowing what a rough "first" this would be for my friend, I agreed.

On the way home that day we stopped for dinner at one of Katie's favorite restaurants. Over dinner, we talked about Katie and how much she enjoyed days like this one with Rayford. This rugged outdoorsman cried and spoke of her with warmth and love. Clearly that day became a stepping stone to overcome his grief and remember Katie with love. That experience has taught me that grief comes in waves on the survivors and that a comforting hand on those days can save them from being swept out with the tide.

Cultivating the seeds of the Gospel. The second reason to continue contact with unchurched families is to cultivate the seeds you planted during the service itself. Often visible acts of compassion (like preparing a funeral dinner) made by the church family show the survivors how the church meets needs. The results of these contacts can be everlasting, as noted in Chapter One.

FOUR WAYS MINISTERS CAN COMFORT

Though there are many ways any Christian can

comfort the mourning after the funeral service, there are some ways that a minister is especially enabled to fulfill. Here are four: provide audio tapes of the memorial service, furnish a manuscript of the funeral address, present a "Letter from Heaven," and refer to the deceased Christian as an example in Sunday sermons.

Provide audio-tapes. This is one of the simplest ways to extend the comfort the family felt from the funeral service. Early in my ministry, I recorded the service only if the family had requested it, but I received so many requests for copies of the message that I now record every one.

It has surprised me how often family and friends want copies of the service. After I spoke at my father-in-law's service, Vic's ice-fishing friend said that he was a retired police officer, an Eagles Club member and had attended hundreds of funerals. "That was the most personal service I have ever attended," he said. "My wife has heard so many funerals about the 'Valley of Death' that she won't come with me any more. Is there any way I can get a copy of the message?"

Fortunately, we had recorded it. I sent him a copy. A few days later I received a thank you card from him. He wrote, "Thank you for sending along the tape of Vic's funeral. My wife and I listened to it the afternoon it came in the mail. Vic was a friend. In a couple months the ice-fishing season will be upon me. When I'm on the lake (with a lot of time for meditation), I will remember him fondly."

Audio tapes of the service also fill a need when some of the family cannot attend the funeral because of distance or health. In such cases, I provide copies to the family and allow them to distribute them.

A Manuscript of the Message. Sometimes the family requests a written copy of the message. Since I preach the personal profile from a handwritten manuscript, creating a manuscript simply means typing it out. Even with the tapes, some people desire a manuscript that they can read and reread it.

Poems and "Letters from Heaven." Some ministers, gifted in poetry, such as Justin Shepard, write personal poetry about the deceased and family. These poems, with a simple rhyme pattern, can be photocopied and shared with the family. Other ministers, like Ray Merritt, write "Letters from Heaven." These letters relay what the deceased Christian might say if he could write the family from his recent vantage point — Heaven. These "Letters" have been so popular that Ray now brings several copies with him to the funeral. What makes these "Letters" comforting is Ray's ability to capture the essence of the deceased's thoughts and words. He only creates these "Letters" for people he was comfortably familiar with.

Speak of the deceased in sermons. When Katie Wild suffered with cancer, she displayed great courage and faith in the face of her disease. Her cheerful, faithful spirit prepared us for her departure. She believed (and so do we) that God could heal her of the cancer. But He did not. Her testimony was amplified by her suffering. She was not healed but still believed.

Her life illustrated that it takes more faith to endure suffering than to enact a healing. Her life showed that sometimes God calms the storm and sometimes He calms His child. Her faithfulness affected her husband too. Months after her death, he underwent quadruple by-pass heart surgery. "Kenn, I'm in a win/win situation," Rayford told me the morning of his surgery. "If the surgery is successful, I win. If it's not, I *still* win . . . ."

These illustrations brought tears to the eyes of Katie's family and friends, yet they were comforted knowing she was remembered fondly by others.

WAYS ANY CHRISTIAN CAN COMFORT

Listening

The Greek New Testament word for "comfort" and "encouragement" is the word *paraklete*, which means "one called along side" — to stand beside someone in their time of need. "Comfort" in this sense means *presence*. Jesus used this word to describe the Holy Spirit, who would be the disciples' Comforter when Jesus would no longer be *present* with them (John 14:16-18). John uses this same word to describe Jesus in I John 2:1. Paul uses it several times in II Corinthians 1:3-7, to show that we must comfort others with the comfort we've received in Christ.

There is a comfort and encouragement that comes simply by being present with the mourner. In part, this entails listening. Mourning people want to share about the deceased. They are hurt when friends treat the deceased's name as taboo. One mother, whose son took his own life just before Christmas, wanted someone to listen to her. To find someone, she had to turn to a support group of other suicide survivors. She said:

> Just talking with and hearing from people who have gone through the same thing was a tremendous help and made me feel normal again. One of the things which was particularly helpful was that we survivors read the letter left behind. Before I joined the support group, I wanted to read my letter and talk about it, but no one wanted to hear it. But people who have gone through this know how important that is and we are willing to listen and share.
> – ("Suicide . . . " by Victor Parachin, The *Lookout*,
> May 3, 1992)

Marjorie Gordon also wrote of the importance of listening:

> To be a comforter — a mourning partner — you don't need to give friends answers. Sit with them, pray with them, walk with them, wait with them. If they ask the inevitable "Why?" your response can be, "I don't know why, but I'll stay with you."
> Listen when the story is told over and over. Don't attempt to solve the problem. Remember the mourning process takes a long time.
> Some people who feel inadequate to meet another's needs respond by withdrawing. They add

to the hurt without knowing it. Their friend is thinking, "Why haven't I heard from him or her?"
–("The Grief Connection," *Christian Standard,* August 11, 1991)

Remember Special Days

During the first year after a death, several special days will renew the grief of loved ones. Marjorie Gordon wrote:

> The tenderness of warmhearted friends helped us on difficult days throughout the year following our loss . . . My uncontrollable tears on Dave's birthday were punctuated with phone calls. On Mother's Day I received a phone call from a friend who visited David's grave that day in the Black Hills National Cemetery in Sturgis, South Dakota. He knew we lived 1,100 miles away. I wanted to tell you there was a fresh-cut red rose in a bud vase and a potted plant with lavender blossoms at Dave's headstone when we arrived. He will never know how important his message was.

Mother's Day, birthdays (both the deceased's and the survivor's), wedding anniversaries, family reunions, Christmas, Thanksgiving, Easter, and the date of the death, all bring with them a renewed sense of loss. Jean Schaefer in "Beyond Sympathy," *Woman's Day,* writes:

> First holidays: These are also difficult times for the recently widowed woman. The first Christmas without her husband, the first time his birthday comes around, are all likely to be bad days. Help

her over them with a phone call, an invitation, a visit or a warm note.

Sunday: Your friend may dread these traditional family days the most. If she's living alone, take her to church and home for brunch. If she has young children, make a Sunday easier by including them in a backyard cookout or a trip to the zoo with your family.

Send Notes And Letters

Your own expressions and words in a note or letter may not be as eloquent as a poem on a sympathy card, but they mean more to the grieving. Notes containing memories of the deceased are often read and reread by the survivors. Phone calls can uplift the grieving on days of sadness, but do not let them replace personal letters. Personal letters are important in the New Testament. If Luke and Acts were written to Theophilus, and if we include Paul's personal letters to Timothy (two), Titus and Philemon, and the letters of John to "the chosen lady" (II John) and Gaius (III John), then over half of the New Testament by volume and eight of the 27 books were written from one Christian to another. Though none of these epistles were written specifically to comfort the mourning, they lift personal letter writing to a higher level. Billions are still reading these letters.

Marjorie Gordon wrote of this important ministry:

Prevent an empty mailbox. For the first three

weeks the mailbox held its daily treasures of comfort — an anticipated refreshment for days still bathed in grief. It was painful when that first supply ran dry.

But there were sensitive friends who knew this was the time to send a booklet, poem, or Scripture verses with some added words of encouragement. Once again, "I'm thinking of you" means so much . . . Two devoted friends sent weekly messages of hope. Letters of comfort arrived through the passing months. It's never too late to write.

Remember That Children Mourn Too

Sometimes the overlooked survivors are the children affected by the death of a relative or friend. Many parents question whether children should attend a funeral or see the grief of their parents. Lois Duncan had shielded her children from her mother-in-law's funeral. In her "What Are Funerals For?" she wrote, "For our children . . . Their grandmother's death is not a reality to them. Last Christmas, our youngest daughter bought Nana a present — 'I saw this and I know how much she likes blue.'

"Our teenage son, preparing to fly to Michigan for the wedding of a cousin, said, 'I hope he brings Nana to the airport.'

"'Honey, Nana is dead,' I said gently.

"'I forgot,' he responded sheepishly.

"Our children are not stupid. On an intellectual level, they know their grandmother is dead. On an emotional level, however, they 'forget.' In their hearts, they harbor the belief that she is in hiding and will someday pop out, shouting 'Surprise.'

"Since my mother-in-law's death, I have discussed funerals with several psychologists, all of whom agree that their function is not just to honor the deceased, but to aid the survivors in purging themselves of grief. Like other rites of passage — graduations, weddings, retirement parties — funerals help us adjust to major life transitions.

"I now believe that I did our children an injustice by not giving them the opportunity to come to grips with the death of their grandmother at her funeral. In my efforts to shelter them from pain, I may have left open an emotional door that they'll have to struggle for years to close. I do not intend to make the same mistake the next time a loved one dies."

Children are especially at risk when it is one of their siblings who died. Elizabeth Richter, author of a book on sibling grief entitled *Losing Someone You Love* wrote:

> In the past several years, experts have begun to look at the emotional impact that sibling death has on sisters and brothers — and many are finding that adolescence may be the worst time of life for grief.
>
> "If I had to pick the family member at greatest emotional risk when a child dies," says Gerald Koocher, staff psychologist at Children's Hospital in Boston, "it would be the adolescent sibling. It's a period when a young person is going outside the family to establish himself as an individual within a peer group. They are trying very hard to escape the family unit. It's not a time when most kids

want to sit down with their folks to talk about feel-ings."

Young children may want to express their love and grief in unusual ways. Sometimes it is best to understand and aid them as they work through their grief. Mayo Mathers told eleven-year-old Landon's story in an article entitled "A Letter For Luke," *Focus On The Family*, November, 1991.

Landon told his mom one day, "I wish I could write a letter to Luke." The mother could see the tears her son was trying not to shed. Nine months before, Landon's friend, Luke, had died suddenly of a brain hemorrhage.

Landon's grief was deep, unreachable. His mother longed to ease his pain, though she could do nothing except hold him as he wept. Maybe, she thought, writing a letter was a good idea. She handed Landon paper and colored pencils. "Tell Luke how much you miss him and how much you love him. Tell him you haven't forgotten him."

Landon wrote the letter. A long one. The com-pleted paper was a work of art. He wrote each line in a different color and carefully drew an elaborate border around the edge. It was a love letter . . . a message from earth to heaven.

Landon folded the paper carefully, tied it to a balloon, and took it to a steep butte. Before they released it, they prayed that God would take it and give it to Luke. When the balloon disappeared through the clouds, Landon whispered reverently, "Did you see that, Mom? God got my balloon."

THE MOST COMFORTING TOUCH OF ALL — If we use all the techniques contained in this book, we will share eloquent stories of the deceased and proclaim the Gospel with power. But if we have not LOVE, we will be as a clanging gong. The most comforting touch of all is the love of God. May they see Christ's compassion in our actions, and The Father's comfort in our eyes. May we become the channel through which God's love flows and His comfort graces their lives.

APPENDIX:
An Anecdote About Heaven

To illuminate the reality of Heaven, Dr. W.W. Winters shared the following story. I use the framework of this story to tell my own experiences with the death of my teen-aged basketball team-mate, my uncle's death (he was mistakenly murdered by thugs who killed several black people at random one night — my uncle was white), and my memories of the Christian deceased.

"When I was a little boy my Bible School teachers taught me about Heaven. They said that Heaven was a city a long way off with streets of gold, walls of precious stones, and twelve gates of pearl — three on the east wall, three on the west, three on the north and three on the south.

"God the Father, Jesus the Son and the Holy Spirit were there. So were men of faith like Moses, Elijah and David. There were lots of other people there too — but to me Heaven seemed so unreal.

"One day my dearest friend, Jean Hill, became sick. Jean — my seven-year-old playmate — had a little red wagon, I had a wooden one and we had coasted down every hill we could find.

"At the hospital, Jean's appendix ruptured and he had the mumps. In a few days he was dead. When they brought his body back in a big black car, I asked my mother, 'Where's Jean?' Without hesitation she answered, 'In Heaven.'

"That afternoon I thought again about Heaven. I thought of the streets of gold, and the twelve pearly gates. God, the Son and the Holy Spirit were there with all the men of faith. There were lots of other people there too. And as I peered through one of the gates I saw a seven-year-old riding his coaster wagon on the streets of gold.

"Ten years later . . . Ray Bollman, my high school friend, played bass drum in the school band, and I played the sousaphone. Ray — four years my senior — signed up with the United States Air Corps in World War II. He was flying an old Liberator bomber — which the fliers called 'the flying coffin' — when his plane went into a flat spin.

"A military guard accompanied his body back to the church where Ray and I had worshiped the Lord together. Later, as we stood at the graveside at Little Blue River Cemetery, I thought about

Heaven . . . .

"I thought of the streets of gold, and the twelve pearly gates. God, the Son and the Holy Spirit were there with all the men of faith. I looked through one of the gates and saw a seven-year-old riding his coaster wagon on the streets of gold and a young man beating his bass drum as the saints went marching in.

"Years later, my father laid smitten with a stroke, as the angel of death floated through the upstairs window of the apartment. The lace curtain moved ever so slightly as if stirred by a breeze through an open window and Dad entered that upper and better kingdom. As I stood there looking out the window, I thought about Heaven . . .

"I thought of the streets of gold, and the twelve pearly gates. God, the Son and the Holy Spirit were there with all the men of faith. I looked through one of the gates and saw a seven-year-old riding his coaster wagon on the streets of gold and a young man beating his bass drum as the saints went marching in. And I saw a quiet man who had stood weekly before the communion table at church and shared the meditation at the Lord's Table. Now he sat and talked with Moses, Elijah and David.

"Then I understood about Heaven."

BIBLIOGRAPHY

Allen, R. Earl. *Funeral Source Book*. Grand Rapids: Baker Book House, 1964.

Blair, Robert. *The Minister's Funeral Handbook*. Grand Rapids: Baker Book House, 1990.

Duncan, Lois. *What Is a Funeral For?* (Pamphlet). National Selected Morticians Resources Inc., 1616 Central Street, Evanston, Illinois 60201, 1986.

Franzen, Janice Gosnell. *The Adventure Of Interviewing*. Wheaton, Illinois: Christian Writers Institute, 1989.

Huron, Roderick. *Christian Minister's Manual*. Cincinnati, Ohio: Standard Publishing, 1960.

Jones, E. Ray. *Standard Funeral Manual*. Cincinnati, Ohio: Standard Publishing, 1991.

Lewis, C.S. *A Grief Observed.* New York: Bantam Books, 1961. (Bantam edition March, 1976)

Mumford, Amy & Danhauer, Karen E. *Love Away My Hurt: A Child's Book About Death* (For Grades 1-6). Denver: Accent Books, 1983. 1-800-525-5550

Murphree, Jon Tal. *A Loving God & a Suffering World.* Downers Grove, Illinois: InterVarsity Press, 1981.

Richter, Elizabeth. *Losing Someone You Love: When a Brother Or Sister Dies.* New York: Putnam Publishing Group, 1986.

Switzer, David K. *The Minister as Crisis Counselor.* Nashville: Abingdon Press, 1986.

White, Willie W. *What The Bible Says About Suffering.* Joplin, Missouri: College Press Publishing, 1984.

INDEX

fying with, 85,86; their perceived needs, 87,88
See also Survivors
Audio tapes: of funerals, 168,169
"Beyond The Sunset": 101,102
Blindness: 153
Biography: significance of, 57,58. *See also* Profile
Bitterness: with deceased, 38; toward God, 119-121,122; over death of child, 145; unresolved, 155,156
Burial Tradition: 101
Cooley, Charles: "Looking Glass Concept of Self," 157
Children: attending funerals, 174-176; grief of, 174-177, *See also* Survivors; Grief; Sibling Grief
Church: involvement of deceased, 54; to grieving, 134,170-175
Comfort: letters to survivors, 27,28,164,173,174; defined, 41,170,171; of Jesus, 71,72
Committal Service: 101,102
Death: effect on community, 16,134,135,; Jesus' empathy, 31,32; bitterness about, 35-38; anecdote "The Door," 88-89; "sleeping," 91-94; definition of, 92; three types, 92,93; Jesus' power over, 95,96; anecdote "The Sting of Death," 98,99; of a child, 99,100,131,132,133,; by disease, 132,133,134; Adam and Eve, 137; murder, 140-143; of infants, SIDS, 143,144. *See also* Accidental Death
Denial: stage of grief, 29
Depression: stage of grief, 28,29; support to, 148
Elijah: 148
Encouragement: *See* Comfort

93; texts, 95; topics, 95; Biblical anecdotes,
96,97; using "outside" stories, 97-100. *See also*
Funeral

Graveside Service: 100-102

Grief: deceased remembered, 18-21; ways to comfort grieving, 24,25,163-177, ; perspective of
death, 24; Jesus' empathy, 24,25,31,32; healing
of, 27,28; stages of grief, 28-30; acceptance of
death, 29,30; can lead to salvation, 31-33;
interview as therapy, 37-39; verbalizing, 38; bitterness with deceased, 37,38; at public viewing,
40,41; the compassion of presence, 41; a poem,
67,68; by Paul, 70,71; by Christians, 70-72;
faith of parent comforts children, 76-77; related
to humor, e4,5; 106,107; guilt over suicide, 147;
post-funeral ministry often inadequate, 167;
comfort of friends, 164-165; of spouse, 166;
grieving traditions, 166; not over quickly, 166;
fluctuates in intensity, 166,167; holidays renew
loss,167; of children, 174-177; of siblings,
174-175; expressed by children, 175-177. *See
also* Survivors

Handicapped: insight from "Empty Egg," 99-100;
valued as individuals, 149,150; salvation of,
151; God's will, 151-153

Hardy, G.B.: 91

Heaven: football anecdote, 76-77

Hobbies: of deceased, 51-53; show Christian
kindness, 75

Holidays: times of renewed grief, 167

Humor: example at funeral, 63; touches broad
spectrum, 107; no jokes, 107,108

Hymns: favorites of deceased, 64. *See also* Music
Idiot Savants: 150
Impersonal Funerals: 18-20
Interview: motivation, 16; of survivors, 35; as
    grief therapy, 37; as catalyst for healing, 38,39;
    whom to, 40; where to, 40; scheduling it, 40;
    conducting it, 41,42; questions to ask, 45;
    humorous stories, 63,111,112; uncomfortable
    with humor, 115-117
Introduction: to funeral message, 58,59-61;
    example, 60,61
"It Is Well With My Soul": 64
Jairus' Daughter: raised by Jesus, 31,96,97
Jargon: of Christians not for funerals, 90,91
Jesus: stories by, 25,26; raised Jairus' daughter,
    31,96,97; empathy with grieving, 30,31;
    comforts, 71,72; power over death illustrated,
    96,97; His own death, 129
Job: 123,124,148
Jokes: 107,108
Jonah: 148
Judas Iscariot: 148
"Last Kiss": the 1961 song's view of death,
    121,122
Laughter: at funerals, 103-105. *See also* Humor
Lazarus: 71,72
Letters: of memories to survivors, 27,28; "Letters
    from Heaven," 169,170
"Looking Glass Concept of Self": 157
Listening: as a comfort, 170,171
Manuscripts: of funerals messages, 73
Mentally Handicapped: *See* Handicapped

127. *See* also Freedom

Natural Laws: transgressed can result in suffering, 131,132

Pastor: *See* Minister

Paul: his grief, 70,71; his testimony, 88

Philippian Jailer: 148

Poetry: "I Need The Quiet," 54; written by minister, 67,169; of deceased, 67,75; an untitled poem about memories, 67,68; from survivors, 68; cold funeral poetry, 68,69; "Should You Go First," 69; "Heaven's Very Special Child," 152,153

Prayer: 61,62; at committal service, 100

Private Viewing: of deceased, 40,41

Prodigal Son: example of the impact of details, 25-27; example of moral freedom, 127,128; as freedom example, 137; illustrates God's compassion, 137,138

Profile: mentioning failures of deceased, 20,65; a recollection, 20,21; using first names, 21; eulogy format, 21,22; pitfalls of, 30,31; benefits of, 31-33; of vocational background, 47,49,63; of service groups, 48; of military service, 48,49; of family relationships, 49-51; of deceased favorite things, 51-53; of hobbies, 52; of deceased's faith, 53-55; significance of, 57,58; formats of, 61,72,73; selecting materials for, 62-72; anecdote of faith, 64,65; victory over failure, 65; personal comments by minister, 65-67; using Biblical stories, 70-72; delivery, 73; how not to idealize the deceased, 73,74; manuscripts, 73; example eulogy, 74-77; for non-

Will of God: confusion about, 121-124; prodigal son, 128; example message dealing with, 136-138; mentally handicapped, 151,152; blindness, 133,134,153

Writing: of deceased, 67,68,93; of family, 67; rewriting errant messages from family, 68; "Success" an essay, 69,70; of deceased to family, 171; to deceased by child, 176,177

SCRIPTURAL INDEX

Old Testament

New Testament